Labour: a party fit for imperialism

ROBERT CLOUGH

IMPERIALISM

COUNTERATTACK · 2

First Published 1992

Larkin Publications
BCM Box 5909 London WC1N 3XX

© Larkin Publications

British Library Cataloguing in Publication Data
A catalogue record for this book is available from the British Library

ISBN 0905400 15 1

Typeset in Bembo and Univers
by Boldface Typesetting & Design

Printed in Great Britain by BPCC Wheatons Ltd, Exeter

Contents

CONTENTS

PART FOUR
Labour and British imperialism since 1951

PART FIVE
Labour and the working class 1918-45

PART SIX
Labour and the working class since 1945

Acknowledgements

This book would not have been written without the collective support of my comrades of the Revolutionary Communist Group. I have borrowed unashamedly from articles they have written in the newspaper *Fight Racism! Fight Imperialism!*; a small group of comrades have read and re-read successive drafts, removing the wilder formulations and helping me to tighten the main arguments that it puts forward. I would like to mention in particular David Reed, for his relentlessness; the advice and comments of Eddie Abrahams, Carol Brickley, Andy Higginbottom and Maxine Williams, and the organisational work of Nicki Rensten.   RC

In memory of
TERRY O'HALLORAN
comrade and friend

Labour's impasse

There are two conclusions to draw from Labour's fourth successive General Election defeat. The first is that only under very exceptional conditions has it ever been able to form a government with a significant majority on its own account. The second is that today, such exceptional conditions would require the political and electoral fragmentation of the Tory Party.

Labour's failure has given rise to much debate on its future. Should it reduce or sever its links with the trade unions? Should it support some kind of proportional representation? If so, should it also establish an electoral agreement with the Liberal Democrats to achieve this end? Should it end its commitment to universal benefits? Such questions have filled the left with dismay, since it regards it as an unquestionable axiom that Labour is a workers' party, and that the links with the trade unions express this class basis. In its view, to sever the connection would be a historic setback since it would leave the working class without any independent representation. It has therefore responded with a deluge of articles to the effect that since the working class is still a majority of the population, the issue should not be whether to break with the unions, but how better to represent them.

This book has a very different perspective. It shows that the Labour Party was created by a small, privileged stratum of the working class in alliance with a radical section of the middle class for the purpose of defending their political interests, and that it is not, never has been, and never will be, a party of the working class. However, the narrowness of this social base amongst the better-off sections of the working class forces Labour to appeal for the votes of the mass of the rest of the working class so that it can present itself as a credible parliamentary force. But this does not make it a working class party, and in any case, the votes of the working class are not enough for it to win an election outright. For that, it needs the votes of a much broader section of the middle class, and only twice has it ever won them: in 1945 and 1966. Every other time it has formed a government it has either been as a minority party or held the barest of majorities.

This different perspective exists because of a different starting point to the rest of the left: that throughout Labour's existence, Britain has been a major imperialist power, and that this has been decisive in determining Labour's political development. The narrow stratum of the working class that formed the Labour Party, an aristocracy of labour made up overwhelmingly of skilled craftsmen, arose during the period of Britain's world industrial monopoly following the defeat of Chartism. During the last quarter of the 19th century, as Britain's ascendancy was steadily eroded by US and German competition, the privileged position of the labour aristocracy depended more and more on crumbs it received from Britain's colonial monopoly. As this too came under challenge, so did the position of the labour aristocracy, and from a force it had hitherto regarded as its ally: the Liberal Party. To defend its interests in these conditions, it needed separate parliamentary representation, and to obtain it, it founded the Labour Party in alliance with a section of the radical middle class. Since the privileged conditions of these better-off sections of the population depended on the maintenance of the British Empire, Labour could not defend the one without supporting the other. It was therefore from the outset an imperialist party.

The left critics of Labour, however, either implicitly or explicitly deny the imperialist character of British capitalism, and as a consequence dismiss any suggestion of a split within the working class. It is the theoretical basis on which they can sustain the myth of Labour as a working class party, and it is consistent with the role the left generally plays, as a protector of the Labour Party when political conditions demand. An example of this was the recent General Election campaign, when the left almost without exception campaigned for a Labour vote despite the fact that the policy differences between Labour and Tory were quite insignificant.

As we shall see, even though Labour was to become a major parliamentary force after the 1918 Representation of the People Act enfranchised the mass of the working class – though excluding women under 30 – these additional votes were insufficient for Labour to win a working parliamentary majority. For this, it would need to be able to reconcile the interests of the mass of the working class with those of both its privileged upper layers and a broad section of the middle class; only in the exceptional conditions of 1945 and the post-war boom would this prove possible. This social-democratic or Keynesian consensus of interests was achieved through the establishment of the welfare state. The end of Keynesianism in the 1970s was a recognition that the economic basis for guaranteeing the privileged conditions of the aristocracy of labour and the middle class whilst simultaneously sustaining adequate living standards for the mass of the working class had disappeared. The relative affluence of the former could now only be maintained at the direct expense of the latter. The current discussion within the Labour Party on 'targeting' benefits reflects this new reality.

Since the turn of the century, the form of British imperialism has undoubtedly changed, although not its substance. With it, the labour aristocracy has also changed, although the division within the working class remains, as craft workers have given way to trade union and labour functionaries, skilled white collar workers and administrators particularly in the public sector. The prevailing political culture of this stratum is completely corrupt. By corrupt, we mean it is indifferent to the destitution and oppression both at home and abroad that is the necessary condition for its privileged and parasitic existence. It is completely undemocratic and slavish in spirit, even when political necessity impels it to declare the opposite. This philistinism has become the hallmark of Labourism; no fitter illustration of its consequence is the fact that our democratic and political rights are so poor that appeals for their improvement make up the majority of the work of the European Court. The left too, drawn as it is particularly from the more affluent sections of public sector workers whose numbers expanded so greatly through the economic boom after the Second World War, have succumbed to this dominant culture, and have become no less corrupt than those they seek to replace: their privileged social position has also determined their political standpoint.

The structure of this book reflects its aims. The first section deals with the rise of the labour aristocracy and its relationship to the mass of the working class, the conditions which forced it to seek independent parliamentary representation, and the early years of its existence until the adoption of its 1918 constitution. The second, third and fourth parts show how Labour has made the defence of the Empire and British imperialism the cornerstone of its political standpoint. The relative extent of these sections is necessary because no other history of the Labour Party has recorded it. From the standpoint of the oppressed masses of the world, however, this was the true face of Labour and its commitment to 'democracy' and 'equality'; what Labour has achieved in defending British imperial interests is of far greater historical significance than any of its paltry domestic accomplishments. The last two parts then examine the relationship of the Labour Party to the mass of the British working class since 1918, showing how Labour has consistently attempted to exclude the latter from political life, and, when workers have attempted to defend themselves, attacked them without compunction using all the resources at its disposal.

The 1992 Election took place against the backdrop of an accelerating industrial, financial and political decline of British imperialism. From being the world's largest creditor nation with net overseas assets worth over £100 billion in 1986, its assets were worth a net £16 billion in 1991 after recovering from being a net debtor in 1990. Tokyo has overtaken London as the world's financial centre. North Sea oil revenues are a fraction of their peak in the mid 1980s. Manufacturing output in 1992 is at most 1 per cent above its 1979 level, and manufacturing investment below. The result is an unprecedented peacetime balance of trade deficit on manufactured goods, in the midst of the longest recession since the 1930s. The Public Sector Borrowing Requirement, currently £34 billion, is being constantly revised upwards, whilst services constantly deteriorate through cuts in real spending. Despite this, or more accurately because of it, Labour proved unelectable. It could not persuade the middle class and better-off sections of the working class to shift their support from the Tories, nor could it offer anything meaningful to the mass of the working class, particularly its more impoverished sections. Indeed, Labour ignored them throughout the election and its aftermath; they now only feature as objects of pity or fear, dismissed as an 'underclass'. However, this so-called 'underclass' is rapidly expanding: 47 per cent of all employees now earn less than the European Decency Threshold. The 'underclass' with its connotation of 'unorganisable rabble', the 'people of the abyss' has in fact become a euphemism for the working class, and expresses how far it has been excluded from normal political life. The Los Angeles riots in 1992 show that an impoverished working class will only accept so much. The issue then becomes: who will represent its interests? Labour certainly will not.

ROBERT CLOUGH, JUNE 1992

PART ONE

The foundation of the Labour Party

1.1 *The rise of the labour aristocracy*

The final defeat of Chartism in 1848 ushered in a period during which British capitalism held unchallenged sway throughout the world. From 1850-75 British capitalism, with the markets of the world under its domination, rapidly expanded and was able to relax the extreme pressure which had been ever present in the 1830s and 1840s. Wages rose and conditions improved especially for the skilled craftsmen who more and more assumed the leadership of the working class. These privileged workers turned aside from Chartism to build up their craft trade unions and co-operative societies. 'The spirit of rebellion died and proposals for radical reconstruction of society were brushed aside.'[1]

During this third quarter of the century, annual rates of industrial expansion averaged 2 to 3 per cent, although the increase in productivity was much greater. So, while wages as a share of national income declined, real wages rose substantially – perhaps by as much as a third. By far the greater part of these increases accrued to a privileged stratum of skilled workers and craftsmen – the labour aristocracy. This stratum, some 10 to 15 per cent of the working class, earned a weekly wage approximately double that of unskilled workers. It organised itself into unions which for the first time had a trained staff of full time

---

1. GDH Cole, *Chartist Portraits*, Macmillan, 1965, p338. This section is drawn from D Reed, 'Marx and Engels on the labour aristocracy, opportunism and the British labour movement', *Fight Racism! Fight Imperialism!* No27, March 1983.

officials, with high subscriptions providing for a range of friendly benefits such as unemployment and sickness benefit. Such unions carried out trade practices which hinged on preventing unskilled workers from getting into the trade.

The co-operative societies developed alongside the craft unions. Those who joined them received a 'dividend in purchase', as well as interest on share capital. Whatever the claims of those skilled workers and others who sponsored such societies, the fact that shares were in the region of £1 each would rule out any benefits for the millions of workers earning 15 shillings (s) or less per week. The labour aristocracy was building for itself a stake within the capitalist system, a fact which soon found a political expression. Already in 1858, Engels was noting that the:

'... English proletariat is actually becoming more and more bourgeois, so that this most bourgeois of all nations is apparently aiming ultimately at the possession of a bourgeois aristocracy and a bourgeois proletariat alongside the bourgeoisie. For a nation which exploits the whole world this is of course to a certain extent justifiable.'[2]

Although sections of the trade union leadership played a significant role alongside Marx and Engels in the establishment of the First International, they were often at loggerheads. The International was a major influence behind the Reform League, which was formed in 1865 to agitate on two demands of the Charter – universal male suffrage and vote by secret ballot. Its standing committee of 12 consisted of six middle class radicals and six workers, of whom three, Cremer, Odger and Howell, were members of the General Council of the First International. However, the influence of Marx and Engels was insufficient to prevent the trade union leaders from compromising with the radical bourgeoisie. In 1866 and 1867, Liberal politicians and manufacturers made substantial donations to the League. In return, the League

---

2. F Engels, *Letter to K Marx, 7 October 1858*, in Marx & Engels, *Selected Correspondence*, Progress Publishers, nd, p132.

qualified its demand for male suffrage with the phrase 'registered and residential', thus deliberately excluding the large mass of labourers, casual workers and unemployed. Marx wrote at the time: 'Cremer and Odger have both betrayed us in the Reform League where, against our wishes, they have made compromises with the bourgeoisie.'[3]

After the passage of the 1867 electoral Reform Act, the English trade union leaders in the League worked secretly in exchange for payments and Home Office bribes to mobilise the working class vote behind the Liberals in the 1868 General Election; two leaders, Cremer and Howell were paid electioneering expenses and £10 each to canvass for the Liberals, leading Marx to comment on the 'so-called leaders of the English workers' who 'are more or less bribed by the bourgeoisie and government.'[4]

The conflict also emerged over the Irish question, when Marx defended the Fenian movement within the International in 1869 and attacked Gladstone for his brutal policies and his hypocrisy. English trade union leaders, including Odger, objected strongly and defended Gladstone, whilst three unions left the International altogether. Despite these defections, the International was able to organise massive demonstrations in support of Fenian prisoners. As Engels said later, 'the masses are for the Irish. The organisations and labour aristocracy in general follow Gladstone and the liberal bourgeoisie'.[5]

The strength of British capitalism allowed the bourgeoisie to make concessions to the working class without threatening its economic or political power, and the labour aristocracy was only too happy to accept. In 1874, Engels summarised the development:

'Wherever the workers lately took part in general politics in particular organisations they did so almost exclusively as the extreme left wing of the "great Liberal Party" . . . In order to get into Parliament the "Labour leaders" had recourse, in the first

---

3. K Marx, *Letter to Becker*, 31 August 1866.
4. K Marx, in *Minutes and Documents of the Hague Congress of the First International*, Progress Publishers, 1976, p124.
5. F Engels, in *Marx and Engels on Ireland*, Progress Publishers, 1978, p460.

place, to the votes and money of the bourgeoisie and only in the second place to the votes of the workers themselves. But by doing so they ceased to be workers' candidates and turned themselves into bourgeois candidates.'[6]

1.2   *British imperialism under challenge*

'Advocacy of class collaboration; abandonment of the idea of socialist revolution and revolutionary methods of struggle; adaptation to bourgeois nationalism; losing sight of the fact that the borderlines of nationality and country are historically transient; making a fetish of bourgeois legality; renunciation of the class viewpoint and the class struggle for fear of repelling the "broad masses of the population" (meaning the petty bourgeoisie) – such, doubtlessly, are the ideological foundations of opportunism.'[7]

Opportunism in England consolidated itself in the last quarter of the century. Although by the end of the period, Britain's monopoly industrial position had disappeared for ever in the face of the rising challenge from Germany, the US and France, it possessed a vast Empire, to which major additions were made in the 1880s and 1890s. The plunder from this Empire was to act as a cushion protecting British capitalism from the full impact of the new competition.

The relative decline of British industry was evident in nearly every branch. Whereas industrial output had grown by 39 per cent in the 1850s, and 33 per cent in the 1860s, the average for the three subsequent decades was to fall to 20 per cent. Productivity, which had risen annually by between 1 and 2 per cent now increased by 0.5 per cent in the 1880s and a mere 0.2 per cent in the 1890s. Individual branches reflected this change: British coal production as a percentage of world

---

6. F Engels, *The English Elections*, in *Marx and Engels on Britain*, Progress Publishers 1971, pp369–70.
7. VI Lenin, *The Position and Tasks of the Socialist International*, *Collected Works* (CW) vol 21, Progress Publishers, p35.

production fell from 51.5 per cent to 29.2 per cent, and of pig iron from 40.5 per cent to 22.1 per cent in the period 1870 to 1900. Pig iron production may have increased by 50 per cent during the period, but German output rose 330 per cent and US output 630 per cent. Steel production told a similar story: British production rose from 1.29 million tons in 1880 (31 per cent of the world total) to 4.9 million tons in 1900 (17.6 per cent); however, in the same period, German production rose from 0.69 million tons to 6.36 million tons, and US production from 1.25 million tons to 10.19 million tons.

The increasing lack of competitiveness of British industry expressed itself in a falling domestic rate of profit; hence profitable investment had to be sought abroad, in the Empire, both formal and informal (see Table 1). The result was an immense accumulation of capital overseas (Table 2).

Such figures if anything underestimate the tendency: GDCF includes investment in housing and public building. It would seem that in the years just before the war, perhaps 80 per cent of capital issues on the London market were destined for overseas. Accumulated overseas investment rose as a percentage of GNP from 73 per cent in 1870 to 139 per cent in 1890, and 164 per cent in 1910, by which time it amounted to about a third of domestic capital investment[9]; again, almost

Table 1[8]

	Gross Domestic Capital Formation (GDCF) as % GNP	Foreign Investment as % GDCF	Foreign Investment as % GNP	Total Capital Formation as % GNP
1870-9	10.5	44.0	4.6	15.1
1880-9	9.2	62.1	5.7	14.9
1890-9	9.7	36.7	3.6	13.3
1900-9	10.6	41.6	4.4	15.0
1904-13	9.4	75.6	7.2	16.6

8. DH Aldcroft and HW Richardson, *The British Economy 1870-1939*, Macmillan, 1969, p120.
9. D Nabudere, *The Political Economy of Imperialism*, Zed Press, 1975, pp113-15.

Table 2   **Accumulated capital abroad** (£000,000) [10]

1870	692	1900	2,397
1880	1,189	1910	3,371
1890	1,935	1913	3,990

certainly, official figures underestimate this proportion. Nabudere estimates that the years 1870 to 1913 saw a capital export of £2,400 million yielding a net income of £4,100 million, and that Britain was able to finance new overseas investment out of the return on old investment. [11]

Quite apart from attracting a higher rate of profit, such overseas investment had other benefits, both direct and indirect. First, it facilitated increased capital exports: £600 million invested in overseas railway building between 1907 and 1914 created a monopoly market for iron, steel and rolling stock; secondly, the consequent improvement in means of communications cheapened the costs of transport and therefore of raw materials and foods.

In addition to its colonial monopoly, British imperialism maintained a maritime monopoly, and a monopoly in the finance and insurance of world trade. The former was reflected in its continued domination of the world shipbuilding industry (see Table 3); the construction of larger

Table 3   **Shipbuilding – tonnage launched** (000s of tons) [12]

Year	UK	Germany	USA	World
1895	951	88	85	1,218
1900	1,442	204	333	2,304
1905	1,623	255	303	2,515
1910	1,143	159	331	1,958

10. *ibid*, p64.
11. *ibid*.
12. *Marxist Study Course, Political Economy*, vol 10a, Lawrence, circa 1932, p41.

ships with improved propulsion systems together with the introduction of refrigeration contributed as much as improved land communications to the cheapening of imported raw materials and foods.

Its financial and insurance monopoly expressed itself in a steady increase in invisible overseas earnings other than from investment (Table 4).

Total invisible earnings from abroad rose from 9.3 per cent of GNP in 1870 to 11.5 per cent in 1890 and 13.6 per cent in 1913, a year when gross private trading profits amounted to only 14.2 per cent of GNP.

Table 4 [13]   (£000,000s)

	Gross National Product	Merchandise Exports	Merchandise Imports	Overall Visible Balance
1870	947	246	279	− 33
1880	1097	290	378	− 88
1890	1389	334	387	− 53
1900	1781	356	485	−129
1910	2050	536	632	− 96
1913	2333	637	719	− 82

	Net Export of Services	Net Property Income From Abroad	Overall Invisible Balance	Overall Current Balance
1870	55	35	+ 88	+ 55
1880	65	58	+121	+ 33
1890	67	94	+160	+107
1900	61	104	+163	+ 34
1910	104	170	+270	+174
1913	121	200	+317	+235

13. Drawn from ed B Mitchell and P Deane, *Abstract of British Historical Statistics*, Cambridge, 1962, pp828-9 and 872-3. The slight discrepancy in the total balance of invisible trade arises from currency transactions.

Throughout this period, the balance of payments deficit on visible trade was more than made up by the rising surplus on the so-called invisibles. In other words, the solvency of British imperialism depended on its colonial monopoly – a feature of its fundamental parasitism.

1.3 *Parasitism, the labour aristocracy and the working class*

Britain's colonial monopoly allowed it by and large to continue to maintain the conditions of the labour aristocracy through the last decades of the century. Although money wages remained fairly constant during this period, there was a significant fall in prices, especially of food, as a consequence of the vast improvement in transportation. Hence real wages continued to rise, especially for the more privileged strata of the working class: by 26 per cent in the decade of the 1870s, 21 per cent in the 1880s, slowing down to 11 per cent in the 1890s. Elie Halevy described the results:

'[the fall in] . . . current prices had enabled a very large body to come into existence among the British proletariat, able to keep up a standard of living almost identical with that of the middle class. The self-respecting workman in the North of England wanted to own his own cottage and garden, in Lancashire his piano. His life was insured. If he shared the common English failing and was a gambler, prone to bet too highly on horses . . . the rapid growth of savings banks proved that he was nevertheless learning the prudence of the middle class.'[14]

The improvements were mainly confined to the labour aristocracy: in 1900, skilled workers could on average expect 40s per week, unskilled workers 20-25s, women workers and agricultural workers 15s. But this only gives part of the picture, since on average unemployment was three times higher for the unskilled than for the skilled worker, and he or she was far more likely to be casually, seasonally or otherwise temporarily employed.

---

14. E Halevy, *History of the English People*, Epilogue Book 2, Pelican 1939, p133.

Poverty and destitution remained the norm therefore for masses of unskilled and semi-skilled workers: in 1911, for instance, it was estimated that 30s per week was the minimum to sustain an adequate family existence, but five million out of eight million male manual workers earned less than this; the average for this five million workers was 22s. Sir Leo Chiozza-Money in his 1905 study, *Riches and Poverty*[15] estimated that 33 million out of a population of 43 million lived in poverty, and of these, 13 million lived in destitution. The benefits of Empire were very definitely confined to an upper layer of the working class.

Not surprisingly trade unionism and political life remained the almost exclusive preserve of this layer. In 1892, out of 14 million people employed in industry and trade, only 1.5 million belonged to a trade union, and less than a million belonged to TUC-affiliates. With the very partial exception of the miners, these were still the old craft unions; the unskilled unions were at this time a negligible force. As a proportion of the workforce, trade union membership changed little until shortly before the war; only in 1906 did it exceed two million. Furthermore, the unions were still by and large benefit societies: the annual expenditure of 100 leading unions on strike pay or lock-out benefit only once exceeded 13 per cent of income between 1899 and 1909; during this period expenditure on unemployment and friendly benefits averaged 60 to 70 per cent.

Suffrage was not quite so sharply restricted, but was still only available to a minority of the working class (and of course still excluded all women): the householding qualification of the 1867 Reform Act had enfranchised an electorate of three million, half of them working class. This was raised to only five million by the 1884 Act when it extended the householder's franchise to the counties; such a property qualification meant that its beneficiaries were again drawn from the labour aristocracy. As the official Labour Party history described the situation in 1900: 'by far the greater part of the working men enfranchised thereby were approaching, or past, their middle years, and, not

---

15. Cited in I Cox, *Empire Today*, Lawrence and Wishart, 1960, p16.

withstanding their memories, they were not the material out of which a Labour victory could be achieved.'[16]

This period then was one of political stagnation. British imperialism could still afford to make concessions to the labour aristocracy, in return for which it expected, and usually got, social peace. The exceptions were the free speech demonstrations in London of the late 1880s, and the explosion of unskilled unionism in 1889-90, particularly amongst the dockers and gasworkers. Both these events drove sections of the working class into an alliance with Marxists and revolutionaries; the fact that many of the dockers were Irish (and a large proportion of their strike committee as well) probably facilitated such a development. Not only would the craft unions with their Lib-Lab politics prove incapable of defending the mass of the working class, they were in fact utterly hostile to the revolutionary methods that the new unions used, especially during the dockers' strike. George Shipton, Chairman of London Trades Council argued: 'When the people were unenfranchised, were without votes, the only power left to them was the demonstration of numbers. Now however, the workmen have votes.'[17] Or, at least, the workmen who really counted for Shipton: it was precisely casual labourers such as dockers who were still excluded from the franchise, and therefore from bourgeois political life and could only express their interests through revolutionary means. However, their alliance with the Marxists could not be sustained under the combined attack of the ruling class and its labour aristocrat allies, and within two to three years, the new unions had lost the majority of their members, falling from 300,000 in 1890 (25 per cent of TUC membership) to 80,000 in 1896. By 1900 they constituted less than 10 per cent of the membership of the TUC. They began to ape the organisational and political methods of the old craft unions in order to preserve themselves, rejecting recruitment amongst the casual and unskilled labourers in favour of those in stable employment, for instance

---

16. Lord Shepherd, in ed H Tracey, *The British Labour Party*, Vol 2, Caxton, 1948, p192.
17. Quoted in T Cliff and D Gluckstein, *The Labour Party – a Marxist History*, Bookmarks, 1988, p9.

municipal gasworkers. In other words, the new unions themselves became corrupted by the prevailing trend of opportunism.

1.4 The Independent Labour Party and the Fabians

Since the passage of the 1867 Reform Act, politics for the privileged workers had been Liberal Party politics, and a few workers, mainly miners, had been elected to Parliament since 1874 on a Liberal ticket. But the competitive pressures on British industry at the start of the 1890s revealed that the Liberal capitalists who dominated the mining and cotton industries were every bit as ruthless as their Tory counterparts elsewhere. And it was the defeat of a strike in the cotton industry in 1892 that led to the first organisational break in the Lib-Lab alliance – the formation of the Independent Labour Party (ILP).

Keir Hardie, who was the prime mover behind the founding conference in 1893, was in favour of organisational independence from Liberalism, but not political independence. Hence the conference rejected the name 'Socialist Labour Party' in favour of 'Independent Labour Party' because 'they had to appeal to the vast mass of workers outside, and not only to Socialists' – in other words, to those skilled workers who possessed the vote but who were still quite happy with Liberalism. More than that, the name was a signal to the Liberals that there were no fundamental political disagreements between the two parties, at least none that might prevent them arriving at electoral agreements, open or otherwise. 'For its theories and its detailed facts', Francis Williams' official history notes, the ILP 'drew mainly upon the Fabian society'[18]; hardly surprisingly, since most of its leaders were Fabians, Keir Hardie and Ramsay MacDonald amongst them.

The constituency of the ILP was identical to that of the contemporary trade union movement – the skilled working class. One commentary quotes a description of a Glasgow branch as typical:

---

18. F Williams, *Fifty Years' March – The Rise of the Labour Party*, Odhams, circa 1950, p104.

'Except for an odd teacher and a few shop assistants, the members were all working men and their wives. For the most part the men belonged to the skilled trades as in England and were nearly always known as exceptionally good and steady working men. They were active trade unionists to a man. The ILP was not attracting as yet what are called the "unskilled workers" . . . '[19]

In Sheffield, 'the unskilled, the irregularly employed and the slum dwellers remained almost completely impervious to the ILP appeal. Party organisers discovered that the "indigent have neither time nor opportunity to think out social problems for themselves".'[20]

Whilst the bulk of the membership was drawn from the skilled working class, there was a substantial proportion drawn from the lower professional middle class: 'The formation of the ILP's internal structure, its political ideas, its leadership and organisers was, in fact, directly and substantially affected by the presence of middle class socialists . . . Although small, this group forged the alliance between the ILP, the Radical Liberals and the TUC, and opened the way for the ILP's parliamentary breakthroughs of the early 1900s.'[21] Middle class socialists might be stretching it: Radical Liberalism was as potent an influence on the ILP as the Fabians. It was not just the case that middle class liberalism played a leading organisational and political role within the ILP: they had the links with a variety of wealthy donors such as Cadbury whose financial donations were crucial to the survival of the Party at the turn of the century.

The Fabian Society, which was to prove so influential with both the ILP and the Labour Party, was an organisation of middle class socialists formed in 1884, although of significance only from the late 1880s. Never numbering more than a few hundreds, it saw its purpose as primarily educational. It consciously rejected the class struggle; indeed, it held the working class in complete contempt, as one of its leading

---

19. S Pierson, *Marxism and the Origin of British Socialism*, Cornell, 1973, p209.
20. *ibid*, p210.
21. C Levy, in ed C Levy, *Socialism and the Intelligentsia, 1880-1914*, Routledge and Kegan Paul, 1987, p136.

figures, Beatrice Webb, argued in 1895: 'judging from our knowledge of the Labour movement we can expect no leader from the working class. Our only hope is in permeating the young middle class man.'[22] And: 'What can we hope from these myriads of deficient minds and deformed bodies that swarm our great cities – what can we hope but brutality, meanness and crime.'[23] In 1911, she was to condemn the Liberals' health insurance scheme for workers as 'wholly bad, and I cannot see how malingering can be staved off... What the government shirk is the extension of treatment and *disciplinary supervision.*'[24]

Initially opposed to independent labour representation, the Fabians accepted it in 1892 in the same period as they started to involve themselves in local government – 'gas and water' or municipal socialism. Their motivation was in part to create an alliance with middle class Radicalism – to 'permeate' it, but also for fear that unless something was done to improve municipal services, there might be terrible consequences, as Sidney Webb wrote in their programme for the 1892 London County Council elections:

> 'The largest city in the world, the capital of the Empire, cannot, in these democratic days, safely be abandoned to the insidious influence of its festering centres of social ulceration. We dare not neglect the sullen discontent now spreading among its toiling millions... Metropolitan reform has become a national if not yet an imperial question.'[25]

By 1901 it *had* become an imperial question, when Webb noted that eight million destitute persons – a fifth of the population – constituted 'not merely a disgrace but a positive danger to our civilisation' and asked 'what is the use of an Empire if it does not breed and maintain in the truest and fullest sense of the word an Imperial race?'. He concluded that it was necessary to introduce a national minimum standard of life

---

22. Quoted in J Callaghan, *Socialism in Britain*, Blackwell, 1990, p37.
23. Quoted in Cliff and Gluckstein, *op cit*, p 18.
24. *ibid.*
25. S Webb, *The London Programme*, Swan Sonnenschein, 1891, p6.

'not merely or even mainly for the comfort of the workers but absolutely for the success of our industry in competition in the world.'[26] This imperialist and racist would, with complete justification, come to be described as 'the intellectual leader of the Labour Party'.[27]

Throughout the 1890s, Fabians, the ILP and radical Liberals were to establish a close alliance through the experience of municipal socialism. The ties were often very close: Ramsay MacDonald, for instance, was a leading figure within both the ILP and the Fabian Society at this time, and had a close political relationship of many years' standing with the Liberal anti-imperialist, JA Hobson. This meant that middle class socialism was to play a vital role in formulating the political standpoint of the Labour Party.

1.5   *The Labour Representation Committee*

The initial response of the craft unions to the ILP was one of hostility. The 1895 TUC Congress approved a number of measures to isolate it. It adopted the block vote to determine policy – the ILP was stronger in the smaller unions – and ended trades council representation, again because of the ILP influence in such local bodies. Lastly, it excluded delegates who were not at their trade; Keir Hardie was now working as a journalist, no longer a miner. However the pressure on British industry continued to grow from the 1890s onwards, forcing a series of confrontations, in which the unions suffered significant defeats: the Amalgamated Society of Engineers (ASE) in 1897 (after a lock-out organised by the Engineering Employers' Federation), and the South Wales miners the following year. The Lib-Lab alliance was no longer sufficient to defend the interests of the labour aristocracy; the 1899 TUC therefore voted to convene a conference to set up a Labour Representation Committee (LRC).

---

26. Quoted in Callaghan, *op cit*, p41.
27. Beatrice Webb in 1917, quoted by H Pelling, *A Short History of the Labour Party*, Macmillan, 1972, p42.

The Conference met in February 1900; delegates came from 65 unions with 568,000 members, and from political organisations such as the Social Democratic Federation (SDF), the ILP and the Fabians. The interests of the labour aristocracy dominated the proceedings: an SDF proposal that there be a 'party organisation separate from the capitalist parties based upon a recognition of the class war' was dismissed out of hand in favour of Hardie's formulation, moved by the general secretary of the ASE, that 'this Conference is in favour of working class opinion being represented in the House of Commons by men sympathetic with the aims and demands of the Labour movement', passed by 102 votes to three. Such representatives were 'to form their own distinctive labour group and act in harmony with its decisions.' In other words, the Committee was to be first and foremost a parliamentary body.

The LRC was formed by a trade union movement which excluded 90 per cent of the working class: there were only about 100,000 organised unskilled workers out of a total of some 10 million. The electorate on which it could depend was again drawn from the upper ranks of the working class, since the majority were still without a vote. By its very nature, it was therefore an exclusive body, formed by the craft unions to represent their interests in Parliament more adequately than the Liberal alliance. It was not until 1906 that the LRC voted for universal male suffrage, and, separately, for women's suffrage on the same terms as men (and then only just, by 446,000 'votes' to 429,000). Parliamentary democracy was still a democracy for the privileged, and the labour aristocracy was in no hurry to change it: 'It is an inescapable fact that the early Labour Party took no more than a passing interest in electoral reform.'[28]

By the turn of the century, the competitiveness of British industry had declined to the extent that now even the labour aristocracy began to suffer deteriorating conditions. Between 1900 and 1910, real wages fell by 6 per cent[29], whilst unemployment amongst trade unionists rose

---

28. In H Tracey, *op cit*, vol 2, p193.
29. Aldcroft and Richardson, *op cit*, p105.

steadily from 2.5 per cent to nearly 8 per cent[30]. The response of the craft unions was, however, supine: the number and extent of strikes fell to a record low in 1904, a fact reflected in the parsimonious sums spent by the unions on strike pay. The Taff Vale judgement of 1901 removing trade union immunity for the consequence of strike action further reduced their strength, although re-inforcing their need for parliamentary representation to offset the shortcomings of the Lib-Lab alliance.

Throughout this period, the Labour Party (as it was called from 1906) played second fiddle to the Liberals. Its main aim became the repeal of the Taff Vale judgement; for that it required a Liberal government. There was no attempt at political independence: Labour MPs were still elected courtesy of pacts with the Liberals, since its electoral base was not adequate to guarantee election if it stood unaided. Ramsay MacDonald had assumed the leadership of the Party from Keir Hardie: as Cole and Postgate put it, 'He had a natural skill in parliamentary tactics . . . his conviction that circumstances required an inflexible support of the Liberals reassured the trade unionists.'[31]. The very meagre reward was the 1906 Trades Dispute Act which restored trade unions' immunity to damages arising from industrial action.

Two years later, the Osborne judgement which prevented unions from paying a political levy threatened the solvency of Labour. Not for five years until the 1913 Trades Dispute Act was the original legal position restored. In the meantime, the Parliamentary Labour Party, by this time consisting of some 40 MPs, acted as a support group indistinguishable from the Liberals, even though from 1910 it held the balance of power. At no point did it offer any opposition: its political dependence, epitomised by its secret electoral pact, was too great.

The last four years before the war have been seen as one of the high points of the British trade union movement. In contrast with the previous decade, resistance to the ruling class offensive was considerable. Strikes of seamen and dockers (1911), railwaymen and miners

---

30. J Kuczynski, *Labour Conditions under Industrial Capitalism*, Muller, 1972, p109.
31. Cole and Postgate, *The Common People 1746-1938*, Methuen, 1938, p447.

(1912) brought millions of workers into action. In Liverpool there was a near insurrection against the army, with Tom Mann in the leadership: he was later gaoled for six months for supporting an appeal to troops not to fire on workers. During this period, the Labour Party and to a large extent the ILP leadership offered only condemnation, particularly of the syndicalist influence of leaders such as Mann. But as one delegate put it to the 1912 TUC: 'Syndicalism really is . . . a protest against the inaction of the Labour Party'[32]. Four Labour MPs (including Arthur Henderson) meanwhile put forward a Bill which proposed making strikes illegal unless 30 days' notice had been given; those who struck illegally or incited others to do so would be subjected to very heavy fines. Although the Bill was condemned by the TUC Parliamentary Committee, it demonstrated that even at this early stage of its history Labour would stand against the working class as a whole. As JR Clynes told the 1914 Labour Conference: 'too frequent strikes caused a sense of disgust, of being a nuisance to the community'[33].

1.6 The 1918 Constitution

Until the 1918 Constitution, the Labour Party was a federation of trade unions, particularly the craft unions, and a small number of political organisations such as the ILP and the Fabians. There were no local parties; the Labour Party was represented locally by branches of the ILP in particular. Such a structure was sufficient for a Party which for all its organisational independence was content to act more or less as an appendage to the Liberal Party:

'The war and the disruption of international socialism had landed the British Labour Party in a position it had not held before. Largely owing to the numerical strength – and the wealth – of the

---

32. Quoted in Cliff and Gluckstein, *op cit*, p47. MacDonald agreed, 'Syndicalism is largely a revolt against Socialism [ie the Labour Party]. Socialism must be Parliamentary or it is nothing.' Quoted in *ibid*, p50.
33. Quoted in R Miliband, *Parliamentary Socialism*, Merlin, 1972, p38.

British trade unions, the Labour Party found itself willy-nilly the leading 'Allied' socialist party and the rock upon which European social democracy was already building its fortress against Bolshevism. Consequently, it appeared necessary to construct a political party appropriate to this industrial support.'[34]

It was not just the numerical and financial strength of the trade unions that would make Labour play this role: it was primarily the fact that Britain would emerge from the war as the leading European imperialist power, and therefore the vanguard of the counter-revolution. However, growing internal unrest combined with the political impact of the Russian Revolution had a further consequence: it forced the ruling class to concede universal suffrage for men over 21 and women over 30. The Representation of the People Bill encompassing this proposal would more than double the electorate (from 8.5 million in 1915 to over 22 million in 1922). Labour's social base amongst the more affluent sections of the working class, and in certain layers of the middle class, would in itself be far too narrow an electoral base to enable it to become a significant parliamentary force in the post-war world. To continue to defend their interests, it would have to broaden its electoral support, and the only constituency it could appeal to was the newly enfranchised section of the working class. Labour had to establish proper local Party organisations which could serve to mobilise that vote; to prevent any challenge to the domination of the labour aristocracy it had to keep such organisations under tight central control.

Under the leadership of Arthur Henderson, a committee was established in September 1917 to draft the constitution; it consisted of four craft union leaders, plus Ramsay MacDonald, Arthur Henderson, Sidney Webb and Egerton Wake, a Party organiser. The ILP were effectively excluded from playing any role, as most of the work of the committee devolved on to Henderson and Webb, the latter now acting

---

34. R McKibbin, *The Evolution of the Labour Party 1910-24*, Oxford, 1973, p91.

effectively as Labour's ideological leader. Their draft proposed individual membership, allowed the unions to retain their block vote, and changed voting procedures for the National Executive Committee (NEC).

Henderson and Webb saw individual membership as a means of recruiting middle class support from both the Fabians and disaffected Liberals in organisations such as the Union of Democratic Control (UDC). In proposing that the conference voted for the NEC as a unit, the draft ended the practice whereby political organisations had an exclusive vote for their reserved seats: now the trade unions could cast their block votes for candidates for all seats. Hence the draft effectively gave the trade union barons complete control over conference policy and the subsequently elected NEC.

A special conference in January 1918 considered and rejected the draft. The trade union leaders' only concern was to minimise the influence of the middle class socialists whom they felt were a major threat, mainly because they were associated with a pacifist position during the war. James Sexton of the Dockers spoke of 'the cranks of the UDC and the Council of Civil Liberties avowedly opposing the policy of the Labour Party', and was echoed by Tom Shaw of the Textile Workers, a bastion of imperialism. Henderson made a further concession: the trade unions would be given 13 out of 23 seats on the NEC rather than 11 out of 21. This was sufficient for a subsequent conference in June to accept it.

Clause 4 of the new constitution, and its elaboration in a programme *Labour and the New Social Order* were to be the basis for its electoral appeal to the working class. Sidney Webb wrote both, and in them restated the basic principles of Fabianism. Clause 4 itself was presented at the 1918 Special Conference, and aroused no interest let alone opposition amongst the trade union barons:

'To secure for the producers by hand or brain the full fruits of their industry, and the most equitable distribution thereof that may be possible, upon the basis of the Common Ownership of the Means of Production, and the best obtainable system of popular administration and control of each industry or service.'

This differs only in form with the founding statement of the Fabian Society, for which Webb was also responsible some 30 years earlier:

'It [the Fabian Society] therefore aims at the reorganisation of Society by the emancipation of Land and Industrial Capital from individual and class ownership, and the vesting of them in the community for the general benefit . . . The Society, further, works for the transfer to the community of the administration of such industrial capital as can conveniently be managed socially.'[35]

Nor was there anything new in *Labour and the New Social Order*: there was no attempt to hide the racist and imperialist prejudices of its author, since they would be shared by the social stratum the party represented. Thus it refers to the 'moral claims upon us of the non-adult races', and to the 'great Commonwealth', which was 'not an Empire in the old sense, but a Britannic Alliance'; whatever it was, 'the Labour Party stands for its maintenance and its progressive development', qualified by the vaguest of phrases, 'on the lines of Local Autonomy and "Home Rule All Round" '[36]. And only an imperialist could declare 'As regards our

---

35. Quoted in E Hobsbawm, *Labour's Turning Point 1880-1900*, Lawrence and Wishart, 1948, pp55-6.

36. *Labour and the New Social Order*, 1918, p22. The extreme racism of the Webbs had been voiced five years earlier in the *New Statesman* in 1913. Commenting on the falling white birth rate, they wrote: 'Into the scarcity thus created in particular districts, in particular sections of the labour market, or in particular social strata, there rush the offspring of the less thrifty, the less intellectual, the less foreseeing of races and classes – the unskilled casual labourers of our great cities, the races of Eastern or Southern Europe, the negroes, the Chinese – possibly resulting as already in parts of the USA, in such a heterogeneous and mongrel population that democratic self-government, or even the effective application of the policy of a national minimum of civilised life will become increasingly unattainable. If anything like this happens, it is difficult to avoid the melancholy conclusion that, in some cataclysm that it is impossible for us to foresee, that civilisation characteristic of the Western European races may go the way of half a dozen other civilisations that have within historic times preceded it; to be succeeded by a new social order developed by one or other of the coloured races, the negro, the kaffir or the Chinese.' Quoted in F Lee, *Fabianism and Colonialism – The Life and Thought of Lord Sidney Olivier*, Defiant, 1988, pp189-90.

relations to Foreign Countries, we disavow and disclaim any desire or intention to dispossess or to impoverish any other State or Nation. We seek no increase of territory'[37], since only an imperialist would feel the need to make such disavowals in the context of possessing the largest Empire the world had known. The programme's call for the introduction of a minimum wage together with an extended unemployment benefit system, the nationalisation of the mines, railways and power supply, and the establishment of a progressive taxation system with some kind of welfare state were the means to attract the working class vote.

However, there were also significant bribes for the professional middle class, whom Webb had always thought would be more interested in socialism than the working class. Thus the document is littered with statements that 'this is not a class proposal', whilst workers are always 'workers, by hand or by brain', as they are in Clause 4.

But the main purpose of Clause 4 and *Labour and the New Social Order* as far as Henderson was concerned was to provide a pole of electoral attraction to the mass of the working class. Labour needed these votes if it were to become a significant parliamentary force let alone form a government.

Some have seen in the 1918 Constitution and programme a break with the past, the culmination of a process whereby Labour could in some way represent the interests of the working class. Thus Miliband describes it as a 'considerable step forward'[38]; Cliff and Gluckstein an 'extraordinary transformation', a 'commitment to socialism', a 'minimal anti–capitalist position', that now must be defended[39]; Coates that it marks a break with the past with its 'enormous' promise and its 'radical

---

37. *Labour and the New Social Order*, p22.
38. Miliband, *op cit*, p62.
39. Cliff and Gluckstein, *op cit*, p54 and p72.

and uncompromising' rhetoric[40]. But its racism and its imperialism? Some things, it appears, are best left alone.

In fact the rhetoric of *Labour and the New Social Order* is no different from that in any Fabian document, so that its 'uncompromising' character depends completely on the eye of the beholder. Its aims go no further than any put forward by the Fabians over the previous 30 years,

---

40. D Coates, *The Labour Party and the Struggle for Socialism*, Cambridge, 1975, p14. Theoretically, the left often attempts to justify its position on the Labour Party by referring to Lenin, particularly his speech on relations between the Communist Party and the Labour Party in 1920, when he argued that 'Of course, for the most part the Labour Party consists of workers, but it does not logically follow from this that every workers' party which consists of workers is at the same time a "political workers' party"; that depends upon who leads it, upon the content of its activities and of its political tactics. Only the latter determines whether it is really a political proletarian party. From this point of view, which is the only correct point of view, the Labour Party is not a political workers' party but a thoroughly bourgeois party, because, although it consists of workers, it is led by reactionaries, and the worst reactionaries at that . . . ' (Lenin, *British Labour and British Imperialism*, Lawrence and Wishart, 1969, p267. All page references in this footnote are to this volume). This is cited by the likes of Cliff and Gluckstein (*op cit*, pp1-2), and Mark Harrison in *Permanent Revolution* (Autumn 1991, p6) to mention but two.

From this, those such as Cliff and Gluckstein or Harrison conclude that Lenin understood post-1918 social-democratic parties such as Labour to be 'capitalist workers' parties' – parties with a working class base, but with a pro-capitalist leadership. Yet nowhere does Lenin ever refer to social-democratic parties (let alone the Labour Party) as 'capitalist workers' parties'; in fact, he was at pains to point out how social democracy by definition was isolated from the mass of the working class, and the defection of these parties to the side of their own bourgeoisie on the outbreak of the First Imperialist War proved this. Lenin arrived at his definitive position in 1916, and expressed it most succinctly in his short pamphlet *Imperialism and the Split in Socialism*. He bases himself explicitly on Marx and Engels, developing their analysis to take account of the emergence of imperialism and inter-imperialist rivalries.

Hence he refers to Engels' writing to Marx in 1881 referring to 'the worst type of British trade unions which allow themselves to be led by men who have been bought by the capitalists, or at least, are in their pay'; and to Sorge in 1889 complaining that 'the most repulsive thing here is bourgeois "respectability" with which the workers have become thoroughly saturated'; or later in March 1891, referring to the skilled unions as 'rich and therefore cowardly'; and, six months later, heralding the failure of the 1891 TUC to overturn the decision of Congress the previous year to campaign for an eight-hour day: 'The old unions, with the textile workers at their head, and the whole of the reactionary party among the workers, had exerted all their strength towards overthrowing the eight-

so it takes a particular flight of imagination to characterise it as an 'extraordinary transformation'. In their apparent anxiety to show that Labour was now a progressive force, these historians have developed a complete blindness to imperialism and racism. However, sensing that all is not all well, they cite a second reason for their claim that Labour is a working class organisation: its links with the unions. As we have seen, however, the unions which founded it as a matter of policy excluded 90 per cent of the working class, and represented only a privileged upper

---

hour decision of 1890. They came to grief . . . and the bourgeois papers recognise the defeat of the bourgeois labour party' (p144).

Lenin seizes on Engels' deliberate phrase 'bourgeois labour party', and uses it consistently from then on. Not 'capitalist workers' party' – this is a self-contradictory nonsense. When England's industrial monopoly and later its colonial monopoly came under challenge, conditions arose where every Great Power could 'bribe smaller strata of the "labour aristocracy." ' 'Formerly a "bourgeois labour party", to use Engels' profound expression, could be formed only in one country, because it alone enjoyed a monopoly, and enjoyed it for a long period. Now the "bourgeois labour party" is inevitable and typical for all the imperialist countries' (p146). And, contrasting the opportunists to the increasingly oppressed masses, he continues 'the history of the labour movement will from now on inevitably develop as the history of the struggle between these two tendencies: for the first tendency [ie of opportunism] is not accidental, it is "founded" on economics. The bourgeoisie has already begotten, nurtured, secured for itself "bourgeois labour parties" of social chauvinists in all countries . . . . The important thing is that the economic desertion of a stratum of the labour aristocracy to the side of the bourgeoisie has matured and become an accomplished fact' (p146-7). This split is irrevocable: 'The social chauvinist or (what is the same thing) the opportunist tendency can neither disappear nor "return" to the revolutionary proletariat' (p148).

He concludes 'Engels draws a distinction between the "bourgeois labour party" of the old trade unions, a privileged minority, and the "great mass", the real majority. Engels appeals to the latter, which is not infected with "bourgeois respectability". This is the essence of Marxian tactics!' (p149), and, driving the point home, states 'The fact is that "bourgeois labour parties", as a political phenomenon, have already been formed in all the advanced capitalist countries, and unless a determined ruthless struggle is conducted against these parties all along the line . . . it is useless talking about the struggle against imperialism, about Marxism, or about the socialist labour movement' (p148).

Lenin was absolutely insistent on the need to recognise the existence of the split within the working class, arguing in some notes written in 1920 against those who spoke of the 'proletariat' as an undifferentiated whole: 'The new and material, the concrete is brushed aside, but they keep on talking about the "proletariat" in general', continuing 'the proletariat, not in general, not in abstracto, but in the twentieth century, after the imperialist war, inevitably split from the upper stratum. Evasion of the concrete,

stratum. By the time the general unions had any influence, their structures also excluded the working class, and their leaders were the 'labour lieutenants of the capitalist class' par excellence. Neither in 1900 nor in 1918 did Labour represent the working class, either politically or socially. Quite the opposite: it was set up to exclude the working class from political life, and ensure that a privileged stratum close to the middle class had a vehicle to defend its narrow, parasitic interests. That this necessarily involved defending Britain's imperial interests will be shown in the next section.

---

deception by means of abstractions (dialectics versus eclecticism) (p207).' In other words, to speak of the proletariat (or working class) in general is to use an empty abstraction, since either term glosses over the existence of the split that imperialism has created in its ranks. But this is a closed book for the left.

The term 'capitalist workers' party' is an open concession to the view that Labour is in some way a working class political party. Hence Cliff and Gluckstein refer to the 'ultra-left insanity' of the CPGB when its 1928 Congress announced 'the Labour Party in 1928 has come out unmistakably as the third capitalist party'. Yet this is quite correct: Labour was the third capitalist party, and always had been. The CPGB argument was more fully developed in a pamphlet published prior to the 1929 General Election entitled *Class against Class*. In it, they argued that: 'The situation in 1929 is entirely different from that of the years prior to the General Strike and the Labour Government of 1924. In the years immediately after the war, the Labour Party, in spite of its anti-working class leaders, was forced by the pressure of the workers into action against the Tories and the Liberals, eg threatened general strike against war on Russia, repudiation of the Versailles Treaty . . . The Labour Party also had not yet become a closely-knit party with a single discipline. It was a federation . . . offering facilities for criticism from within.'

However, the advent of the 1924 Labour Government had completely purged the Labour Party of any susceptibility to working class influence, and with it what remained of a federal structure. As the pamphlet concludes, the leadership had 'tied the trade unions to the Tories and the Liberals under the banner of Mondism and transformed the Labour Party from a federal organisation to a single party with a capitalist programme under the banner of "Empire and Mondism" '. (Quoted in N Branson and B Moore, *Labour-Communist Relations 1920-51*, Part 1, Our History Pamphlet, 1990, p50.)

Whatever the mistakes of the CPGB in this period, its characterisation of the Labour Party in the period of the 1929 General Election was most certainly not one. It is in the same vein as Luxemburg's description of German Social Democracy as 'a stinking corpse', which Lenin approvingly quoted in *The Proletarian Revolution and the Renegade Kautsky* (CW vol 28 p241, Progress, 1965). This pithy characterisation is in utter contrast to Cliff and Gluckstein's flabby and long-winded sophistry.

From the Dublin Lock-Out in 1913 to sending in troops to the Six Counties in 1969, Labour has always supported British occupation of Ireland

PART TWO

The Labour Party and British imperialism 1900-45

The Labour Party, then, was established to defend the privileged interests of an upper stratum of the working class in alliance with a section of the middle class. These privileges depended on the relative strength of British imperialism; defending them therefore meant defending British imperialism. Throughout its history, Labour has proved itself equal to the task. In its politically corrupt world, 'democracy' became a particularly debased word: always used to denounce revolution, it was never applicable to the near 500 million people of the British Empire until it became politically convenient. Labour's hypocrisy and racism are founded in the material existence of the stratum which created and built it, since their political rights and privileges depended on the denial of those self-same rights to hundreds of millions of others. It therefore cannot be reduced to the inadequacies of individual leaders, or to weaknesses and deficiencies in the ideological foundations of Labourism. The terms 'trade union bureaucracy' or 'labour bureaucracy', which the left borrows from liberal sociology to analyse Labour, precisely obscure this political reality. In short, the Labour Party and British imperialism are inseparable: neither could survive without the other.

With very few exceptions, histories of the Labour Party refer very rarely to the existence of the British Empire or British imperialism. This may not be surprising for the more reactionary accounts such as those of Henry Pelling or Francis Williams (see Bibliography). However, there is no excuse for those who write from the left – Ralph Miliband, James

Hinton, David Coates or Cliff and Gluckstein from the Socialist Workers Party (SWP); one can only say that they too have been caught up in Labour's web of corruption. To give an example, the index in Cliff and Gluckstein's book has no entries against either 'empire' or 'imperialism', but finds room for four under 'tokenism'. The reason for this is not hard to find: membership of the left is by and large drawn from prosperous layers of public sector workers that British imperialism could afford to support in ever-increasing numbers in the post-1945 period. These 'respectable' people therefore find no relationship between the Labour Party on the one hand and the imperialist character of British capitalism on the other, because they have no interest in looking for one.

It is as well to recall what constituted the British Empire, and the resources it contained. There was Ireland, of course, a source of cheap food and cheap labour. India, with nearly ten times the population of Britain, and worth some £120 million net per year in the 1930s: it supplied over a million troops in each of the two world wars. Malaya with its rubber and tin. Swathes of West Africa with cocoa and palm oil, and much of East Africa. The West Indies with its sugar. The settler Dominions – Canada, Australia and New Zealand; the mineral wealth of South Africa. Then there was the informal empire: most of Latin America prior to the First Imperialist War; Egypt and Palestine; Persia with its oil. After 1918, more ex-German colonies, and Iraq with its oil. These were the victims on which the British imperialist parasite gorged itself: approximately 500 million people, the overwhelming majority of whom were kept in destitution if not starvation, who had no control over their destinies, and in whose name Labour was to govern on three occasions.

2.1   *From the Boer War to 1914*

The foundation of the Labour Representation Committee took place as British imperialism found itself bogged down in an increasingly brutal war against the Boer settlers of the Transvaal. The issue it posed was quite clear to the radical wing of the Liberal Party led by JA Hobson: it was a struggle by British finance for control over the diamond and gold resources of southern Africa. In this struggle, the Radical Liberals took the side of the Boers. The ILP, under the influence of the Radicals, adopted a similar standpoint, arguing that the Government wanted 'to promote a war of conquest . . . in the interest of unscrupulous exploiters'.[1] Keir Hardie was particularly forthright; the war was:

'. . . a Capitalists' war, begotten by Capitalists' money, lied into being by a perjured mercenary Capitalist press, and fathered by unscrupulous politicians, themselves the merest tools of the Capitalists . . . As Socialists, our sympathies are bound to be with the Boers.'[2]

However, the trade union aristocracy was split down the middle. Some stood completely with the ILP; others were more ambivalent, tinging their opposition with gross anti-Semitism – John Burns, earlier a leader of the dockers' strike, preferring the Boer leader Kruger to 'the horde of Jews and greedy gentiles who ha[d] corralled the old fellow in'.[3] Still yet others, such as Havelock Wilson of the Seamen and Will Crooks of the Gasmen were strongly jingoistic. The 1900 TUC adopted an anti-war resolution, but as Poirier points out: 'patriotic sentiment and the fact that war production usually meant increased pay and more jobs could not be ignored, and the resolution passed by only a small minority'.[4] Congress the following year refused to debate the issue further, a fact that was taken to indicate tacit support for the war. This kind of response was already leading Hobson to the conclusion that: 'in many towns, the most important trades are dependent upon government employment or contracts; the imperialism of the metal and shipbuilding centres is attributable in no small degree to this fact.'[5]

---

1. ILP 1900 Annual Report, quoted in P Poirier, *The Advent of the Labour Party*, George Allen and Unwin, 1958, p101.
2. Quoted in B Porter, *Critics of Empire – British Radical Attitudes to Imperialism in Africa 1895-1914*, Macmillan, 1966, p128.
3. Quoted in Poirier, *op cit*, p102.
4. *ibid*, p103.
5. From JA Hobson, *Imperialism*, quoted in VI Lenin, *Imperialism, The Highest Stage of Capitalism*, CW vol 22, p279.

The Fabians were the one group which adopted an unequivocally pro-imperialist stance, and their overall position was set forth by GB Shaw in his pamphlet *Fabianism and Empire*. Shaw described the aim of the Fabians as the 'effective social organisation of the Empire', and argued that: 'the notion that a nation has a right to do what it pleases with its own territory, without reference to the interests of the rest of the world, is no more tenable from the international socialist point of view – that is, the point of view of the 20th century – than the notion that a landlord has a right to do what he likes with his estate without reference to the interests of his neighbours.'[6]

Not that Hobson was an unconditional defender of the right of nations to self-determination:

'Assuming that the arts of "progress", or some of them, are communicable, a fact which is hardly disputable, there can be no inherent natural right in a nation to refuse that measure of compulsory education which shall raise it from childhood to manhood in the order of nationalities.'[7]

It was a position shared by the ILP: Ramsay MacDonald, who had been a close colleague of Hobson since the early 1890s, drew heavily on his Liberal friend in a series of articles published in 1901. In them he proclaimed that: 'so far as the underlying spirit of Imperialism is a frank acceptance of national duty exercised beyond the nation's political frontier . . . [it] cannot be condemned.' Indeed: 'the compulsion to expand and to assume world responsibility is worthy at its origin.'[8] This allowed a completely pragmatic attitude to British imperialism in particular:

'The question of Empire cannot be decided on first principles, so far as this country is concerned. We have a history, and it is an Imperial one.'[9]

---

6. Quoted in Porter, *op cit*, pp116-17.
7. From JA Hobson, *Imperialism*, quoted in Porter, *op cit*, p231.
8. Quoted in *ibid*, pp185-86.
9. *ibid*, p189.

It was not possible to: 'rewrite history, to undo evil . . . we have gone so far in our imperialist history that we can hardly look back. We can be guided in our future work; we cannot re-cut and re-carve the past.' In the meantime, it was sufficient to: 'rule our Empire wisely' and 'to take more interest in its welfare.'[10]

MacDonald would later intervene in a debate on 'socialist colonialism' at the 1907 Stuttgart Congress of the Second International, supporting the resolution that: 'Congress does not, in principle and for all times, reject all colonial policy, which, under a socialist regime may have a civilising effect' on the basis that 'we must have the courage to draw up a program of colonial policy . . . Capitalists cannot do all they want to do in the sphere of colonial policy, for they are generally submitted to the control of Parliaments.'[11] In this he merely echoed the position of the German Social Democrat Bernstein, who had argued that: 'We must not assume a purely negative standpoint . . . on the question of colonial policy, but instead must pursue a positive socialist colonial policy. We must get away from the utopian idea that aims at simply leaving the colonies . . . The colonies are there. We must put up with this fact. A certain guardianship of cultured peoples over non-cultured peoples is a necessity, which should also be recognised by socialists.'[12]

MacDonald's colleague Philip Snowden, ILP member for Blackburn, put this view into practice when he was moved to applaud government support for the development of cotton plantations in East Africa in 1905: 'As a member for a Lancashire constituency which consumes more raw cotton than any other country in the world I cannot but look with approval on the proposal to grant a loan for the development of cotton growing in East Africa.'[13]

---

10. *ibid*, p189.
11. Quoted in R Fox, *The Colonial Policy of British Imperialism*, Lawrence, 1933, p111.
12. Quoted in *Manifesto of the Revolutionary Communist Group*, Larkin, 1984, p42. The German socialist, David, was even more forthright: 'Europe needs colonies. She does not even have enough. Without colonies, from an economic point of view, we shall sink to the level of China.' Quoted in R Fox, *op cit* p110.
13. Quoted in Porter, *op cit*, p297.

The influential cotton unions had always had an interest in Empire: in 1896, they campaigned against a decision by the colonial government in India to impose tariffs on cotton imports from Britain, and only gave up when an equivalent duty was placed on Indian imports into Britain. When this was lifted in 1915 as a sop to the Indian bourgeoisie, they unsuccessfully renewed their campaign, arguing: 'there is doubtless an existing body of opinion in favour of a measure of protection for native industries. But these classes . . . are in no position to speak for the people of India at large, who are our wards, and towards whom we have great responsibilities.' Snowden was again prominent in their support. [14]

In 1921, as author of *Labour and the New World*, Snowden was to state that there were 'inexorable limits to the right of self-determination.' Using China as an example, he argued that it had no right to 'deprive the rest of the world of access to her material resources' [15], and, almost paraphrasing Shaw's *Fabianism and Empire*, he concluded:

'By no moral right may the ownership and control of the natural and material resources of a territory be regarded as the absolute monopoly of the people who happen to be settled there.' [16]

In practice, no section of the British labour movement considered the interests of the dispossessed black peoples of southern Africa. The Boer War was the only occasion on which a substantial section of the labour aristocracy was to adopt a position which was remotely opposed to British imperialism. The Radical Liberals created the space for this in their denunciation of the British financiers. It was however their swansong: the growth of banking capital and its merging with industrial capital was already undermining the Liberal Party as the representative of manufacturing industry. The future of the Radicals lay in an alliance with the labour aristocracy, but in conditions where British imperialism's colonial monopoly would be increasingly under

---

14. Quoted in PS Gupta, *Imperialism and the British Labour Movement 1914-64*, Cambridge, 1975, p43.
15. P Snowden, *Labour and the New World*, Waverly, 1921, p289.
16. *ibid*.

challenge. In these circumstances, neither could afford themselves the luxury of such demonstrations of opposition: their privileged existence was mortgaged to British imperialism. Their attitude to the 1913 Dublin Lock-Out showed this.

2.2 The 1913 Dublin Lock-Out[17]

Like the 1889 dockers' strike, the Dublin Lock-Out of 1913 involved an alliance between revolutionaries (Jim Larkin and James Connolly) and the mass of the disenfranchised working class. The response of the labour aristocracy was to be no less hostile. In 1907, Snowden had already defended the Government's 'employment of the military to quell disorder' when troops had been used in an attempt to defeat the unionisation of Belfast dockers under Larkin's leadership. At the TUC Congress on 1 September, six days after the Lock-Out started, James Sexton called for support for the Dublin workers 'black as James Larkin might be, and James Connolly too'. The day before, police had attacked strikers on a demonstration, killing two. 50,000 people attended the funeral of one of the victims on 3 September, the procession being guarded by Irish Transport and General Workers Union (ITGWU) squads bearing make-shift arms. Throughout September, unofficial sympathy strikes took place on the British mainland, which leaders such as JH Thomas of the Railwaymen did their successful best to stop.

At the end of October, the TUC sent £2,000 for distribution amongst 'affiliated unions'; the ITGWU did not receive a penny because it was not an affiliate of the British TUC. In mid-November, Larkin made a direct appeal to British workers in a series of meetings up and down the country. He had been released from a seven-month gaol sentence after serving just 17 days due to an active campaign. Calling for national strike action, he spoke to thousands of workers – 5,000 in Manchester's Free Trade Hall, with 20,000 outside. Under this pressure, the TUC convened a special Congress on 9 December. The day after this

---

17. Much of this section is drawn from D Reed, *Ireland: the Key to the British Revolution*, Larkin, 1984, pp30-39.

announcement, Larkin along with George Lansbury (editor of the *Daily Herald*) denounced the Labour Party and the TUC for their inaction: 10,000 came to the Albert Hall to hear Larkin, again leaving thousands waiting outside.

The breaking point came when Larkin called on workers through the *Daily Herald* to tell their leaders to stand for trade unionism, and that: 'they are not there as apologists for the shortcomings of the capitalist system'. The response was immediate. Havelock Wilson issued a manifesto denouncing Larkin and the methods of the ITGWU, whilst Snowden described strikes as 'demoralising'. Larkin told a mass meeting in London: 'I am not going to allow these serpents to raise their foul heads and spit out their poison any longer.'

At the TUC Conference, after Connolly presented the case for the Dublin workers, speaker after speaker, led by Ben Tillett, once one of the most radical leaders of the dockers, denounced the strike, condemning Larkin's unfair treatment of British trade union officials. Tillett went on to ask Congress to affirm its confidence in TUC officials to negotiate an honourable settlement, effectively over the heads of the ITGWU. Larkin responded against a growing uproar, denouncing the leaders for their betrayal. Tillett and the rest of the leadership had their way: isolated, the Dublin workers were eventually starved into submission. The opportunism of the privileged leadership of the British working class had triumphed.

2.3   The First Imperialist War

The advent of World War was to show how far Labour had travelled since the Boer War. Although Britain was in no immediate military danger, or indeed under threat of attack in those first four days of August 1914, there was no doubt that it needed to settle accounts with the German challenge to colonial monopoly. Two days before the declaration of war on 4 August, massive demonstrations had heard Labour leaders denounce the impending threat and issue calls to resist it, in line with the policy of the Second International. But by 5 August, the trade union MPs – some 35 of them – had deserted to the ruling class, leaving but five ILP MPs, MacDonald, Hardie and Snowden amongst them, to wring their hands in dismay, supported by an equally small number of Liberals.

Within days, the Labour Party had called an industrial truce, and shortly after an electoral truce as well, placing its national organisation at the disposal of a recruitment campaign. Union leaders such as Ben Tillett acted as recruiting sergeants, vilifying conscientious objectors. Havelock Wilson denounced ILP calls for a negotiated peace, saying: 'some of you would be content to meet these men! [the Germans] You would take the blood-stained hands of murderers in your own'. [18] A manifesto issued by the Labour leadership stated: 'The victory of Germany would mean the death of democracy in Europe . . . Until the Power which has pillaged and outraged Belgium and the Belgians, and plunged nearly the whole of Europe into the awful misery, suffering and horror of war is beaten there can be no peace.' [19]

That the defence of democracy required an alliance with Tsarist reaction did not trouble such leaders at all. In February 1915, Labour convened a meeting of Allied Socialists which adopted a resolution declaring: 'The invasion of Belgium and France by the German armies threatens the very existence of independent nationalities, and strikes a blow at all faith in treaties. In these circumstances a victory for German imperialism would be the defeat and the destruction of democracy and liberty in Europe.' [20] Given Britain's colonial monopoly, the reference to 'independent nationalities' was typical of Labour's corrupt defence of privilege. Pamphlets issued by Radicals such as ED Morel and Norman Angell showed the predatory nature of these treaties and the imperialist interests they expressed. But such opposition was isolated as the official labour movement sanctioned the most appalling slaughter the international working class had ever known to defend British imperialism.

In May 1915, Arthur Henderson, who had replaced MacDonald as

---

18. Quoted in Cliff and Gluckstein, *op cit*, p59.
19. Quoted in Tracey, *op cit*, vol 1, p105.
20. *ibid*.

leader of the Parliamentary Labour Party, joined a coalition government which included Edward Carson as Attorney General and eight other Ulster Unionists. Truly by their friends shall ye know them! It was less than two years since Carson had openly prepared for military struggle against the Liberal's Home Rule Bill for Ireland. Now Labour was in alliance with those it had once denounced as the antithesis of 'democracy'. Imperialism needed Labour's involvement in order to mobilise the working class for war, to ensure a plentiful supply of recruits eager to defend 'democracy', and to impose discipline on the workforce left behind.

Although there were some within the ILP who were to maintain a courageous opposition, their leaders were not amongst them – not once did they oppose war credits. MacDonald himself called for the prosecution of the war to the end: 'Victory must therefore be ours. England is not played out, her mission is not accomplished ... We must go straight through ... the young men of the country must, for the moment, settle the immediate issue of victory. Let them do it in the spirit of the brave men who have crowned our country with honour in the times that are gone.'[21] An ILP Manifesto published in late 1914 urged members to 'carry on a general propaganda of socialism "though not dealing specifically with the war" '.[22] The change since 1900 was spelled out by Keir Hardie:

> 'A nation at war must be united, especially when its existence is at stake. In such filibustering expeditions as our own Boer War ... where no national danger of any kind was involved, there were many occasions for diversity of opinion ... With the boom of enemy guns within earshot, the lads who have gone forth to fight their country's battles must not be disheartened by any discordant notes at home.'[23]

---

21. Quoted in Cliff and Gluckstein, *op cit*, p21.
22. Quoted in R Fox, *The Class Struggle in Britain*, vol 2, Lawrence, 1932, p22.
23. Quoted in Miliband, *op cit*, p44.

Meanwhile, the Irish people had chosen a different side. The ITGWU immediately denounced the war as imperialist, and organised protests against it. The fruits of Connolly's agitation came with the proclamation of the Irish Republic on Easter 1916. The reaction from the British movement was unequivocal. On behalf of the ILP, *Socialist Review* pontificated: 'We do not approve armed rebellion at all, any more than any other militarism or war . . . Nor do we complain against the Government for having opposed and suppressed armed rebellion by armed force.'[24] Another ILP publication, *Labour Leader*, declared that Connolly was 'criminally mistaken', whilst George Lansbury described the uprising as a crime against the Irish people. After the suppression of the revolt, the War Cabinet authorised the execution of its leader; when news reached Parliament of Connolly's death, Arthur Henderson led other Labour MPs in a spontaneous round of applause.

When Labour dealt with the possible post-war fate of the Empire, it was quite clear that there was to be no change, especially in Africa. A December 1917 'Memorandum on War Aims' explained: 'it is impracticable here (ie in Africa) to leave the various peoples concerned to settle their own destinies', describing them as 'non-adult races'.[25] In a more specific reply to Bolshevik peace proposals in January 1918, the Party stated: 'Nobody contends that the black races can govern themselves. They can only make it known that the particular government under which they have been living is bad in some or all respects, and indicate the specific evils from which they desire liberation.'[26]

ED Morel, an ex-Radical Liberal who was on the advisory committee which formulated Labour Party colonial policy at the time, had written in 1911: 'in no period of time which can be forecast, will the condition of West African society permit of the supreme governing power being shared by both races.'[27] In other words, tutelage was to be indefinite.

---

24. Quoted in D Reed, *op cit*, p59.
25. Quoted in Gupta, *op cit*, p53. The Memorandum was itself drafted by the ubiquitous Sidney Webb.
26. *ibid*.
27. *ibid*.

Racism was the very stuff of such politics; in April 1920, Morel wrote an article for Lansbury's *Daily Herald*, following the French Army's deployment of Moroccan troops during their occupation of Germany, in which he referred to France 'thrusting her black savages into the heart of Germany'. He went on to talk of the 'barely restrainable bestiality of the black troops', which had led to rapes and consequent injury and death for 'well-known physiological reasons'. The *Daily Herald* commended the article; a follow-up pamphlet was distributed at the 1920 TUC under the auspices of the Standing Order Committee, whilst Morel was able to involve well-known leaders like JR Clynes, Robert Smillie, Robert Williams and Ben Turner in his campaign.[28]

The end of the war led to an explosion within the working class, stimulated by the success of the Russian Revolution. Mutinies in the Army, massive strikes in industry, and a meteoric rise of trade union membership to eight million served notice to the ruling class that it would have great difficulty in enforcing its will. Yet Labour, in co-operation with the trade union leadership, tried to ensure that the effect of such challenges was kept to a minimum. In September 1918, its Executive had despatched Henderson to an Inter-Allied Conference of Allied Labour and Socialist Parties with instructions not to 'approve or condemn Allied intervention' which British imperialism was leading in Russia, but to accept it 'as an accomplished fact'. In the absence of any organised opposition, they were able to get away with a tacit acceptance of British intervention. Later, in April 1920, dockers led by Harry Pollitt amongst others boycotted the *Jolly George* when they learned that it was to be loaded with arms to be used against the Red Army. In August, a specially convened conference of the Labour Party and TUC issued blood-curdling threats as to their response if British imperialism carried out its evident intention to send troops to support Polish aggression against the Soviet Union. The Polish victory shortly afterwards avoided the need to put this to the test.

---

28. For example, Callaghan, *op cit*, p93.

2.4   *The Labour Party and the Second International*

The Second International[29] had collapsed at the outbreak of the war, as its leading parties rushed to the defence of their respective imperialist ruling classes. The major exception was the Bolshevik Party which stood by the decisions made by the International in various conferences before 1914 calling for mass working class action against war if it should break out. The defection of the leaders of Social Democracy caused Rosa Luxemburg to describe the International as a 'mouldering corpse', and Lenin to fight for a new, Third International. In March, 1918, a conference of Allied socialist parties – the open chauvinists – set up a committee to resurrect the Second International. Its first Conference took place in Berne in February 1919.

From the outset, the Labour Party, which had been an insignificant force in the pre-war International, played a leading role. Henderson was its first Chairman, and Ramsay MacDonald its Secretary. The Conference declared that 'in full agreement with all previous Congresses of the International, the Berne Conference firmly adheres to the principles of democracy'. Hence, it proclaimed itself to be fully in favour of self-determination, but what this meant in practice was left 'to a future conference'! Its next Conference at Geneva in early 1920 defined the 'Political System of Socialism' in a resolution that drew heavily on *Labour and the New Social Order*, and so made no reference to the existence of the class struggle. In between the conferences, it had set up a Permanent Commission of seven members, three of whom were British. 'The headquarters [of the International] were placed in London, and in effect the British Labour Party took charge of its affairs.'[30]

---

29. The Second International was formed in 1889 as the successor to the First International of Marx's day which had dissolved in 1876. It was a loose amalgam of a variety of socialist parties and trade unions, which included open opportunists as well as revolutionary currents. Several Congresses, including the last one held at Basle in 1912, had declared the intention of the International to oppose any imperialist war by international action; August 1914 showed the extent of imperialist corruption when all the leading parties bar the Bolsheviks supported 'their' ruling class in the slaughter of the First Imperialist War.

30. GDH Cole, *A History of Socialist Thought*, vol 4, Part 1, Macmillan, 1958, pp329-30.

The founding Congress of the Third International had taken place in March 1919; at its second, in August 1920, it established stringent conditions of admission to exclude not just the open chauvinists, but also the social-pacifists who wanted to reconstruct a united International. These last (including the ILP at a time when MacDonald was Secretary to the Berne International) set up the Vienna Union, or Two-and-a-Half International, in February 1921. From the outset, both the Second and the Two-and-a-Half Internationals were determined to isolate the Russian Revolution: led by the Labour Party, the former counterposed its empty concept of 'democracy' – which naturally excluded all the colonies – to that of 'Bolshevik dictatorship'. Its main attack on the new-born Soviet Union was over Georgia.

The October Revolution had no immediate echo in Georgia, where a Menshevik government had been set up. Following the Brest-Litovsk peace treaty of April 1918, German troops moved into Georgia. Despite the fact that the Georgian Mensheviks had wanted to continue the war against Germany, they loyally co-operated with the occupying army, the Menshevik President Zhordania declaring in September to the German commander: 'It is not in our interests to lower the prestige of Germany in the Caucasus.'[31] Within two months, he had to swallow these words, as the British moved in from Persia in the wake of the German defeat, occupied the main Trans-Caucasian towns and 'left the Georgian Menshevik government in office under their supervision.'[32] By January the following year, Zhordania could say of the British commander: 'General Walker ... proved to be the first person that understood the state of affairs in our country.'[33], whilst another leading Menshevik was saying: 'I assume that our republic will co-operate with the Allied countries in their fight against the Bolsheviks, with all the means at its disposal'[34]. The Georgian Mensheviks were as good as their word: throughout 1918 and 1919, they supported the counter-

31. Quoted in Trotsky, *Social Democracy and the Wars of Intervention*, New Park, 1975, p24.
32. GDH Cole, *op cit*, vol 4, Part 1, p206.
33. Quoted in Trotsky, *op cit*, p45.
34. Quoted *ibid*, p25.

revolutionary armies of Kolchak and Denikin, and, in 1920, allowed the defeated Denikin forces to regroup under Wrangel. Zhordania himself made it quite clear: 'I know that our enemies will say that we are on the side of the imperialists. Therefore I must say most emphatically: that I prefer the imperialists of the West to the fanatics of the East.'[35] Domestically, the Mensheviks suppressed the Georgian Communist Party, put down numerous peasant uprisings particularly amongst the national minorities, and even engaged in a little war with Armenia over some disputed territory. In February 1921, the Red Army put an end to this bastion of counter-revolution.

However, Georgia was to become a *cause celebre* for the chauvinists. Self-determination may not apply to the colonies, to India or Ireland, but it was the absolute right of Georgia. Kautsky, MacDonald, and Ethel Snowden made visits to Georgia on behalf of the Second International to view the achievements of Georgian Mensheviks, using it to denounce the Russian Revolution. In May 1922, at a meeting of representatives of all three Internationals chaired by the imperialist Tom Shaw, those from the Second and Two-and-a-Half Internationals denounced the 'occupation' of Georgia, and demanded the restoration of the Mensheviks, whilst rejecting any joint campaign against the imperialist Versailles Treaty. In May 1923, the depleted forces of the Two-and-a-Half International merged with the Second to form the Labour and Socialist International (LSI) with Tom Shaw as one of the two joint secretaries and Henderson remaining as chair. The headquarters remained in London 'where Arthur Henderson and the British Labour Party could keep a vigilant eye on its doings'[36]; apart from the Austrian Adler, 'the Administrative Committee that took charge of the International's day-to-day affairs was made up entirely of British members'.[37]. The British grip on the International ensured that it took no position on the issue of colonialism, least of all British colonialism, whilst constantly demanding a Menshevik restoration in Georgia. As

---

35. Quoted *ibid*, p54.
36. Cole, *op cit*, vol 4, Part 2, p684.
37. *ibid*.

one Communist wittily characterised the LSI position: 'There is another country to which the parties affiliated to the LSI must give special attention, ie, to Georgia . . . The liberation of this country from the Bolshevik yoke constitutes one of the chief aims of the LSI. Every true social-democrat has two countries: his own, and Georgia.'[38] On the other hand: 'The LSI, whose activity is based on the idea of international solidarity and which opposes every nationalism except that which defends itself, is pledged to combat with special energy the Asiatic and African nationalism of the colonial and semi-colonial people.'[39] The LSI was a pawn in the hands of the Labour Party, defending the Versailles imperialist order and British colonialism in particular against the growing unity between the Russian Revolution and the anti-colonial struggle.

2.5 Labour and Ireland 1920-21[40]

Labour viewed the renewed struggle for Irish independence as it always had done: from the standpoint of protecting Britain's imperial interests. *Labour and The New Social Order* recognised 'the claim of the people of Ireland to Home Rule, and to self-determination in all exclusively Irish affairs', and demanded that a 'wide and generous measure of Home Rule should be immediately made law and put in operation.'[41] This meant rejecting any settlement leading to an independent republic. In June 1920, the Labour Conference modified this standpoint, demanding 'free and absolute self-determination' for the Irish people, even if by a narrow majority.[42]

The situation was that the Irish people already had their own assembly – the Daíl Eireann, a constitution – the 1916 Proclamation and the 1919 Daíl Democratic programme, for which they were fighting the terror of the Black and Tans. The issue was therefore not one of rights,

---

38. G Valetzki in *Labour Monthly*, October 1925, p596.
39. *ibid*, p599.
40. Again, this section draws on D Reed, *op cit*, pp64–72.
41. *ibid*, p22.
42. Quoted in D Reed, *op cit*, p70.

but of acknowledging the *de facto* existence of the Republic. This Labour refused to do because the Daíl Eireann was in practice laying claim to the whole of Ireland, which Britain was not prepared to concede. In the meantime, it opposed the terror on the grounds that 'under such conditions it is practically impossible to bring the Irish Republican Army to bay . . . Executions and torture are not deterrents; they have indeed, the opposite effect.' [43] This was to become a familiar Labour refrain: if it ever made a show of disagreeing with British imperialism it would not be over aims, but on the brutality of its means, and then not out of concern for its victims, but out of fear that it might be counter-productive.

Labour's position was made clearer in a 1920 report from a Commission chaired by Arthur Henderson, which declared that: 'It is impossible to treat Ireland as a separate country from Great Britain for military purposes. An invasion of Ireland would be an invasion of Britain . . . the two islands should form a single unit for all war-like purposes.' [44] In December 1920, it arrived at its definitive position, which was for the withdrawal of troops and for the election of a constituent assembly which would work out 'without limitations or fetters, whatever constitution for Ireland the Irish people desire, subject only to two conditions – that it affords protection to minorities and that the Constitution should prevent Ireland from becoming a military or naval menace to Great Britain.' [45] In practice, this conceded both the need for partition and for a continuing military occupation.

The 1920 TUC met in September, as Terence MacSweeny, Mayor of Cork, neared death on hunger strike in Brixton prison. The TUC approved the sending of two telegrams to the Government, but JH Thomas as President of Congress refused to allow MacSweeney's sister to address it, evidently because she might call for some meaningful action. Sitting in the public gallery when he announced the decision, she shouted 'traitors' at the Congress and walked out. [46] 'Traitors' indeed:

---

43. Quoted *ibid*, p69.
44. Quoted in R Fox, *The Colonial Policy of British Imperialism*, p109.
45. Quoted in D Reed, *op cit*, p70.
46. From the Trade Union Congress 52nd Annual Report, 1920, p355.

next year, when Partition was agreed, and the Treaty came before Parliament, it took a Communist MP, Shapur Saklatvala, to force a division and record any opposition to it. Henderson's party had indeed proved a 'bulwark against revolution', and the Irish people could well ponder Snowden's comments on the 'inexorable limits to the right to self-determination': Ireland was not Georgia.

2.6   Labour and India 1919-23

By the end of the war, India was in as much turmoil as Ireland. Britain had plundered it of manpower, finance and food resources. The first three years of the war had cost it £270 million: part of this was used to fund the one million strong army it provided to British imperialism, and which was crucial in preventing the German Army from occupying the Channel ports in its 1914–15 campaign. But it also included a forced loan of £100 million, which George Lansbury was later to describe as a 'gift'.[47] And, at a time when two-thirds of the population was starving, Indian exports of wheat and cereals amounted to 2.5 million tons in 1917, and even more in 1918.

The mutinous state of the Indian Army, and the impact of the Russian Revolution, meant that some political concessions to the nascent Indian bourgeoisie were needed to stabilise imperialist rule. The Secretary of State for India, Edwin Montagu, touring India in 1918, described the 'seething, boiling, political flood raging across the country.'[48] He proclaimed the Government's aim as: 'the gradual development of self-governing institutions with a view to the progressive realisation of Responsible Government in India as an integral part of the British Empire.' Together with the Indian Viceroy, Lord Chelmsford, he prepared a report on the necessary constitutional changes to buy off at least one section of the Indian bourgeoisie.

---

47. G Lansbury, *Labour's Way with the Commonwealth*, Methuen, 1935, p51. It is difficult to conceive of what £100 million meant in 1915; certainly it is at least £10 billion in today's terms, and probably over £20 billion if it is assessed as a proportion of GDP.
48. *ibid*, p54.

The Montagu-Chelmsford reforms were based on a plan devised by an Empire Federationist, Lionel Curtis. Responsibility for three departments, those of education, health and local government, would be transferred to elected ministers, but only at a provincial level: national structures would remain unchanged. Even then, the vital department of finance would remain under the control of the Indian Civil Service. There would be a franchise: three million out of 350 million people would be allowed the vote. The progress of these reforms would then be reviewed after a period of ten years. At the request of the Labour Party, Curtis produced a pamphlet explaining his proposals for use by Labour candidates in the 1918 General Election. 'At present', he wrote, 'the number of people who could understand the vote is small. To grant full responsible government outright ... would place government in the hands of a very few.'[49] At the Berne Congress of the Second International in 1919, Labour was to state its support for Home Rule, and claim that these reforms indicated that 'British policy has been tending in this direction for some time.'[50]

However, such 'reforms' were irrelevant to the mass of the Indian people. Famine stalked the land: estimates as to the number who died from a combination of flu and starvation in 1918-19 range from 12 to 30 million. The countryside was a tinder-box, and, starting in the heartland of the cotton industry, Bombay, a massive strike-wave spread throughout the major industrial centres. The only response was repression: a Bill enacting new measures to combat 'sedition' and 'terrorism' proposed by the Rowlatt Committee took effect in March 1919. On 13 April, a meeting against the Rowlatt Act took place in Amritsar in the Punjab. Under the command of General Dwyer, a column of troops opened fire on the peaceful crowd. 379 people were murdered, 1,200 injured.

Under Gandhi's reluctant leadership, the campaign spread throughout early 1921: spontaneous non-payment of taxes started in some areas; more ominously for the Indian landlord class, peasants

---

49. Quoted in Gupta, *op cit*, p42.
50. Quoted in R Fox, *The Class Struggle in Britain*, *op cit*, Part 2, p68.

began a rent strike. In January, Gandhi wrote to Chelmsford, stating that unless all prisoners were released, and the Rowlatt Act repealed, he would authorise a campaign of mass civil disobedience . . . in the District of Bardoli, home for a mere 87,000 people. Shortly after irate peasants stormed the police station in the village of Chauri Chaura and burned 22 policemen to death. On 12 February, Gandhi unconditionally called off the campaign complaining that: 'the country is not non-violent enough', advising 'the cultivators to pay land revenue and other taxes due to the government, and to suspend every other activity of an offensive nature', and ordering the peasants that withholding rent to the landlords was 'injurious to the best interests of the country.'[51]

During all of this Labour was guided by the notion that India, like Ireland, was above politics; it would differ from the Government, but only in detail, not in substance. JH Thomas, to become Labour's first Colonial Secretary within three years, was of the opinion that 'It is a fact that, at the moment, there would be very few people in India among the natives who would understand the significance of the power to vote. This means that responsible government, as in Canada, could not be arranged just now.'[52] In January 1922, at the height of the struggle, the TUC and the Labour Party joined together to issue a statement saying nothing about self-government, but stating 'While realising the necessity of preserving order in India, the Council deplores the political arrests . . . but deplores no less the action of the non-co-operators in boycotting the parliamentary institutions recently conferred upon India by which grievances should be ventilated and wrongs redressed.'[53]

2.7 The 1924 Labour Government

The December 1923 Election returned 192 Labour MPs who, with 157 Liberals, held a majority over the 258 Conservatives. With the failure of

---

51. Quoted in R Palme Dutt, *India Today*, Left Book Club, 1940, pp316-17. Much of the material on the Indian struggle is drawn from this, undoubtedly the best book on the history of the Indian struggle.
52. JH Thomas, *When Labour Rules*, Collins, 1920, p139.
53. Quoted by Clemens Dutt, *Labour Monthly*, September 1926, p545.

Tory diplomacy in Europe, the Middle East and India, British imperialism needed to adopt a less militaristic and more conciliatory guise: a Labour Government would suit it admirably. If matters got out of hand, it could be speedily brought down; in the meantime, it could learn how to administer the imperial machine. The Liberals agreed to support a minority Labour Government – consummating the alliance between the labour aristocracy and the middle class. JH Thomas was put in charge of the Colonial Office, announcing that he was there to ensure there was no mucking about with the Empire. As if to underline the point, Lord Chelmsford, now retired from India, was given the Admiralty, Sidney Olivier, a Fabian and former colonial governor was given the India Office, Lord Haldane, a Liberal imperialist who had supported the Taff Vale judgement, became Lord Chancellor, and the Tory Lord Thompson was put in charge of the RAF.

Labour had consistently denounced the Versailles Treaty even if it had prevented any action against it; as late as 1923, MacDonald had declared that 'there will never be peace so long as the Versailles Treaty is in existence', arguing that 'pursuing the will-o'-the-wisp of reparations is the great curse of every country.'[54] Within 48 hours of coming into office, as he was later to boast, MacDonald had accepted the Dawes report in its entirety, and had made the forcing of it on to the German working class the chief object of his European policy. The Dawes report, prepared on behalf of American bankers, accepted the premise of Versailles: that Germany should pay war reparations – it merely re-scheduled them over a longer period. And what if Germany wouldn't accept? 'She must accept. We shall make her accept. We must have some settlement,' MacDonald declared at a meeting of the PLP.[55] At the 1924 London Conference, despite French misgivings, Germany did accept: Labour had committed itself to the Treaty it had denounced for the previous four years.

Given the make-up of the Cabinet, it is not surprising that there was indeed no mucking about with the Empire. Far from it. JH Thomas was

---

54. Quoted by 'UDC', *Labour Monthly*, February 1925, p104.
55. *ibid*, p109.

all for exploiting the 'incalculable riches of our splendid possessions.' MacDonald as both Prime Minister and Foreign Secretary, stated, in case there was any doubt, that:

'I can see no hope in India if it becomes the arena of a struggle between constitutionalism and revolution. No party in Great Britain will be cowed by threats of force or by policies designed to bring Government to a standstill; and if any section in India are under the delusion that is not so, events will sadly disappoint them.'[56]

On 6 February 1924, Olivier made his policy on the 1919 India reforms absolutely clear: to change them for the establishment of full responsible government:

' . . . would be worse than perilous, it would be big with disaster to the people of India . . . The programme of constitutional democracy . . . was not native to India . . . It was impossible for the Indian people or Indian politicians to leap at once into the saddle and administer an ideal constitution . . . The right of British statesmen, public servants, merchants and industrialists to be in India today was the fact that they had made the India of today, and that no Home Rule or national movement could have been possible in India had it not been for their work.'[57]

No wonder *The Times* found these views 'reassuring' and 'deserving of full recognition'. And as if to underline its position, the Government sanctioned the passage of yet more repressive legislation, the Bengal Ordinance, which allowed for detention without charge let alone trial.

---

56. Quoted by MN Roy, *Labour Monthly*, April 1924, p207.
57. Quoted in *ibid*, p209. Olivier had been Governor of Jamaica between 1907 and 1913 at a salary of £5,000 per annum – some £500,000 in today's terms – and had been a leading Fabian since the late 1880s, resigning over their support for British imperialism in the Boer War. However, he held no shrift for the rights of the colonial people, arguing: 'I have said that the West Indian negro is not fit for complete democratic citizenship in a Constitution of modern Parliamentary form, and I should certainly hold the same opinion with respect to any African native community.' Quoted in F Lee, *op cit*, p117.

In the Middle East, the Labour Government consolidated British imperialism's grip on some of the prizes won from Versailles. It rubber-stamped a treaty with Iraq which gave Britain total control over Iraqi fiscal, foreign and military policy, and allowing it to garrison the country and set up air bases. It sanctioned the use of the RAF to support the campaign of the British puppet government against the Kurds, explaining that because the RAF dropped warning-leaflets ahead of the bombs and gas, no significant injuries took place. Lord Thompson was rather more frank about this than the Under-Minister for Air in the House of Commons when he remarked in November that the effects of air attacks in Iraq were 'appalling', and that panic-stricken tribesmen 'fled into the desert where hundreds more must have perished from thirst . . . The British Air Force in Iraq was the cement which kept the bricks together.'[58]

Finally, the Government refused to accede to Egyptian claims on either the Suez Canal or the Sudan, the latter to the great relief of the cotton unions. For all its pious support for the League of Nations, it declined the proposal of the Egyptian leader Zaghlul Pasha to submit the issue of the British military occupation and control of the Suez Canal to arbitration by the League. MacDonald himself made clear that he adhered to the view that 'absolute certainty that the Suez Canal [would] remain open in peace as in war for the free passage of British ships [was] the foundation on which the entire defence strategy of the British Empire rests.'[59] For the next 30 years, British control of the Suez Canal was to remain a *sine qua non* for the Labour leadership. Zaghlul Pasha, who only accepted office in the belief that a British Labour Government would support Egyptian independence remarked that MacDonald's position was not new but:

> 'What was new to Egypt was that the policy was approved by a Labour Government which had always been opposed to imperialist principles.'[60]

---

58. Quoted in Clemens Dutt, *Labour and the Empire*, CPGB, 1929, p12.
59. Quoted in Gupta, *op cit*, p98.
60. Quoted in *Labour Monthly*, October 1929, p620.

The first Labour Government lasted nine months; its work on Dawes and the Middle East complete, it was summarily despatched. It had demonstrated a fitness for office which was to be remembered five years later; on no issue of imperial defence had it been found wanting. The issue was not whether it was constrained by its minority position: it had determinedly pursued the interests it had been placed in government to advance.

2.8 Empire Socialism

Whilst Britain had retained its position as the dominant European imperialist power, its underlying industrial strength was even less assured than it had been in 1914. Although it had made substantial gains from the carve-up at Versailles, especially in the extension of its informal empire in the Middle East, it did not address the fundamental problem of antiquated manufacturing plant and the resultant low level of productivity. In 1923, British exports of manufactured goods were in real terms 73 per cent their 1913 level, whilst French and US manufactured exports stood at 117 per cent and 148 per cent.[61] In real terms, production in the years 1921-26 averaged 80 to 88 per cent of its pre-war level.[62] Noting that 'A larger number of workers is employed today than before the war, but for a less total production,' Dutt concluded:

> 'What the decline in production reveals is that the productive workers are being thrown on the scrap-heap, while an ever increasing proportion of the working force of the nation is being consumed in unproductive parasitic occupations.'[63]

Net property income from abroad throughout this period averaged £200 to £250 million per annum; although in real terms this was less than half the immediate pre-war rate, it still amounted to 50 per cent of

---

61. R Palme Dutt, *Socialism and the Living Wage*, CPGB, 1927, p39.
62. *ibid*, p40.
63. *ibid*, p41; emphasis in original.

the level of the gross trading profits of private companies. And capital continued to flood abroad: Dutt cites an *Economist* report which analysed new capital issues between 1921 and 1926 under a variety of headings, and showed that of £1,904 million new capital, only £431 million was invested in home industry; the bulk of the rest went abroad. 'Parasitism was becoming a deadly growth on the productive forces of the metropolis'.[64]

Labour expressed particular concern at British imperialism's overall fragility, and the left in particular began to express support for Imperial Preference: that the Empire be consciously used as a protected market for the export of British goods. Thus John Wheatley declared 'Within the British Empire we have a nucleus of unity; therefore I am opposed to any policy of wrecking it.'; he went on to argue that 'Whatever we think of [it], our duty as members of the Labour Movement is to see how we can utilise it to serve our purposes.'[65] Lansbury agreed with him during a parliamentary debate on the issue, during which David Kirkwood declared:

> 'I am all out for cementing the British Empire . . . We are all out for universal peace. There is nothing that can accomplish that better than cementing the British Empire.'[66]

That 'cement' was something the Iraqi people had had first-hand experience of. This trend of Empire Socialism had other exponents: Tom Johnston, who voted with Lansbury, Kirkwood and about 20 other left MPs for Imperial Preference, argued that: 'In some socialist circles – but these are smaller and fewer than they were a dozen years ago – there is a fixed belief that this Empire is an engine of grab and oppression *and that it is and can be nothing more*.'[67] The 1925 Labour Party

---

64. R Fox, *The Colonial Policy of British Imperialism*, p36.
65. Quoted in S MacIntyre, *Imperialism and the British Labour Movement in the 1920s*, CPGB, 1975, p17.
66. Quoted in Clemens Dutt, *Labour and the Empire*, *op cit*, p13.
67. Quoted in JR Campbell, 'Must the Empire be Broken Up?', *Communist Review*, 1924, p218.

Conference adopted Empire Socialism, whilst the following year, the Hobsonian radicals on the Empire Policy Committee of the ILP 'welcom[ed] the possibility of closer economic relationships between the British nation and the various parts of the Commonwealth.'[68] This new twist to socialist colonialism was to achieve full expression with the 1945-51 Labour Government.

2.9 *Labour and China 1927*

Labour's bipartisan approach to imperial diplomacy continued through the years between the first two Labour Governments, as its attitude towards China demonstrates. From the mid-1920s, Britain's dominant position in China was threatened on the one hand by US imperialist interests (against which Britain attempted to ally with the nascent Japanese imperialism), and on the other by rising Chinese Nationalist and Communist movements. The period was marked by the constant despatch of British warships and troops to safeguard British naval bases and extra-territorial concessions, many won following the Opium Wars of the 1830s, with Labour either directing operations, as it did in 1924, or giving eager support. One such incident took place in August 1926, when after a shipping scuffle outside the Yangtze town of Wanhsien, a British gunboat bombarded the town, killing about 500 people. Sir Austen Chamberlain publicly thanked MacDonald for the support he gave to the Government during the episode. In June 1925, a joint Labour Party/TUC resolution argued that the 'point' had not yet 'been reached' where Chinese independence be recognised and British troops withdrawn; this followed an incident the previous month where British marines had fired on and killed a number of demonstrators at Shameen, near Canton.

In 1926, an article in the ILP journal *New Leader* under the title 'Ah Sin at War with himself' referred to the struggle of the Chinese people as like 'our weary old Wars of the Roses', and expressed puzzlement at why 'any human should among the indistinguishable millions of

---

68. Quoted in Macintyre, *op cit*, p18.

China care to risk life and all'[69] in the course of it. The article, with its references to 'Chinks', fully expressed what Palme Dutt described as 'the utter boorish self-centred indifference to every living human struggle, that is the heart and soul of the imperialist psychology in the labour aristocracy and the petty bourgeoisie... looking on with contemptuous indifference to the curious incomprehensible inferior races.'[70]

Early in 1927, a massive strike movement in Shanghai led to a number of incidents when Chinese workers attempted to reclaim the British concession, only to be fired on by British troops. Similar incidents took place in Hankow and Canton, where over 50 people were killed. 20,000 troops were despatched to deal with the threat from the Shanghai uprising; MacDonald argued that: 'the Chinese masses must not be mealy-mouthed as to the consequences of massing on the streets', and added: 'We have to turn to Mr Chen [the Chinese bourgeois nationalist leader] and say "your nationalist demands have our complete support, but we must warn you that if you cannot control mobs no effort of ours will be able to prevent trouble or keep those nationalist demands to the foreground." '[71] JH Thomas was of the opinion that it was better to send a big army than a small one, and went on: 'For some unknown reason, the negotiations have broken down... It is not statesmanlike or patriotic to hamper the Government in a question involving war and peace, or to attempt to make party capital out of the question'. He 'urged' Mr Chen to accept the agreement Britain was forcing on the Chinese people.[72] Meanwhile, George Lansbury in his *Lansbury's Labour Weekly*, also referred to the 'Chinese mobs', and stated: 'we owe a vote of congratulations to our comrades in the navy' for their role in the Hankow incident.[73]

The Shanghai strike movement developed into an insurrection, which was brutally put down by the bourgeois nationalist Kuomin-

---

69. Quoted in *Labour Monthly*, March 1927, p141.
70. *ibid*.
71. Quoted *ibid*, p138.
72. Quoted in *League Against Imperialism, China's Appeal to British Workers*, 1927, p3.
73. Quoted in *Labour Monthly*, March 1927, p139.

tang, aided and abetted by British and Japanese troops. For the left, George Lansbury asked whether there was not some power 'or any way to persuade the Japanese to use some other part of China to attack the Chinese?', for, as he explained, 'white people have lost faith in armaments and force and now want to depend on justice, truth and righteousness.'[74] Hundreds of thousands of Chinese workers died in the 1927 Shanghai massacres, leaving the various imperialist powers in possession of their concessions, and Britain the most powerful amongst them. No wonder that Tom Mann, returning from a visit to China in 1927, wrote of the Chinese people:

> 'They have no illusions about the Chinese capitalists, but the greatest curse, they declare, is the foreign imperialist, and in this they are undoubtedly right; and of all the imperialist forces in China beyond any question Great Britain is the worst.'[75]

2.10   *Labour and India 1927-31*

In late 1927, the Tory Secretary of State for India, Lord Birkenhead, decided to bring forward the statutory review of the progress of the Montagu-Chelmsford reforms in order to guarantee Tory control of the Commission that would carry it out. With the complete eclipse of the Liberals at the 1924 Election, Labour had become the Loyal Opposition; this meant it would be entitled to seats on the Commission. In negotiations with MacDonald on its composition, Birkenhead's aim was to exclude any Indian representation, whilst MacDonald's was to ensure the presence of at least two Labour members. Both achieved what they wanted, and MacDonald over-ruled NEC objections on the absence of any Indians. The two Labour nominees were Clement Attlee and Steven Walsh, the latter a notorious imperialist.

The enabling act setting up the Commission under the Chairmanship of Sir John Simon was rushed through Parliament by Christmas 1927.

---

74. Quoted in H Rathbone, *China*, CPGB, 1930, p13.
75. Tom Mann, *Labour Monthly*, August 1927, p488.

All sections of the Indian nationalist movement were outraged. The Indian TUC passed a motion demanding that Labour 'withdraw its members from the Simon Commission', and resolved that it itself would boycott it. Its President, Chaman Lal, protesting against what he described as MacDonald's 'imperialist proclivities' went on to say 'All classes are aghast at the betrayal by the Labour Party. The Simon Commission will register the middle class imperialist verdict.'[76] Pandhit Nehru, on behalf of Congress told the NEC: 'I am authorised to state that the action of the Labour Party, in not withdrawing its members from the Commission, and trying to effect some kind of compromise, is not supported by any responsible party in India.'[77]

The Simon Commission including Attlee arrived in India in February 1928, to be greeted by a general strike; three demonstrators were killed in a demonstration in Madras. As it proceeded around the country, it was greeted with mass demonstrations, strikes and riots. The Indian working class played a leading role: a colossal strike movement in 1928, with over 30 million days lost, was accompanied by a 70 per cent growth in union membership, and the massive growth of the revolutionary Bombay Girni Kardar or Red Flag Union, with 65,000 members. Meanwhile the 1928 Labour Conference debated a motion opposing the Commission. Fortified by a TUC report which attacked the middle class leadership of the Indian trade union movement, the conference trounced opposition by three million votes to 150,000. No wonder Shapur Saklatvala reported for the *Daily Worker*:

'It has been well-known for some time that the Commission would have a hostile reception from the Indian workers, who view it as the latest weapon of British imperialism . . . When the Bombay workers burned the effigy of MacDonald in the streets along with that of Lord Birkenhead and others, they showed that they viewed the Labour Party as nothing more or less than the willing hirelings of British imperialism.'[78]

---

76. Quoted in Sehri Saklatvala, *The Fifth Commandment*, Manchester Free Press, 1991, p387.
77. *ibid*, p388.
78. *ibid*, pp391–92.

British imperialism was given breathing space by a split in the Indian National Congress at the end of 1928: whilst the left wanted an immediate campaign for independence, Gandhi and the bourgeois wing made any campaign conditional on a British refusal to accept self-government by 31 December 1929. Imperialism had a year in which to prepare. In March 1929, all the most prominent leaders of the Indian working class, including the entire leadership of the Red Flag Union, were arrested and taken to Meerut, detained on a charge of 'attempting to deprive the King-Emperor of the sovereignty of India'. At a crucial stage in the liberation struggle, the working class movement had been decapitated. At the 1929 Labour Conference, a resolution was put calling for the release of the Meerut detainees; Drummond Shiels replied that, 'the Government accepted full responsibility for their present position'; and whereas the Government 'were in favour of the utmost freedom of speech in India consistent with the preservation of public order . . . they took that attitude on the broad principles applicable to every civilised community, but they also took it in the interests of the uninformed humble people of India.'[79] The motion was defeated by a majority of ten to one.

The election of the Labour Government in May 1929 made not the slightest difference to British policy, either as far as the Meerut prisoners were concerned, or in terms of any offer of self-government. Far from it: Labour was called into office, again with Liberal support, to continue the same policy but to serve it up in a dressing of socialist and democratic phrases. As to its imperialist credentials, there was no longer any doubt; as a demonstration of its *bona fides*, Snowden's statement just before the election that Labour would continue to insist on the German payment of war reparations was worth 'hundreds of thousands of votes to us' according to Mrs Snowden.

The end of December came and went without any response from Gandhi, although there were vast demonstrations on Independence Day, 30 January 1930. In the meantime, the Government took the

---

79. Quoted in *Labour Monthly*, November 1929, p682.

precaution of detaining the leading left-wing nationalist Subhas Bose. Then Gandhi announced a march on Dandi by a select band of followers to make salt in defiance of the Government monopoly, to be followed by a campaign of non-co-operation. On 6 April, Gandhi made his salt and the movement exploded once more, as peasants interpreted non-co-operation to mean non-payment of rent as well as taxes. The town of Peshawar fell into the hands of the people following hundreds of deaths and casualties at the hands of loyal troops. But one incident stood out:

'Two platoons of the Second Battalion of the 18th Royal Garwhali Rifles, Hindu troops in the midst of a Moslem crowd, refused the order to fire, broke ranks, fraternised with the crowd, and a number handed over their arms. Immediately after this, the military and police were withdrawn from Peshawar; from 25 April to 4 May the city was in the hands of the people.' [80]

At Sholapur in Bombay, the workers took over the administration for a week. Under Labour's direction, the response of the Government was brutal. Ordinance followed ordinance, creating a condition akin to martial law. Congress was banned in June, and Gandhi arrested. In the 10 months up to April 1931, between 60,000 and 90,000 people were arrested. Physical terror was the norm: 'The records of indiscriminate *lathi* charges, beating up, firing on unarmed crowds, killing of men and women, and punitive expeditions made an ugly picture.' [81] Between 1 April and 14 July alone, 24 incidents of firing had left 103 dead and 420 wounded; by the end of June, the RAF had dropped over 500 tons of bombs in quelling the disturbances.

The Simon Commission reported in June 1930 offering no significant concession, merely fuelling the anger. In an effort to break the impasse, Labour convened a 'Round Table Conference', inviting representatives from the three British parliamentary parties, some Indian merchants, industrialists and landowners and various feudal puppets from the

---

80. R Palme Dutt, *India Today, op cit*, p332.
81. *ibid*, p334.

Indian princely states. Opening it in January 1931, MacDonald declared that: 'I pray that by our labours, India will possess . . . the pride and the honour of Responsible Self-Government'[82] – an offer which was to serve as a bait to Gandhi, but which committed the Government to nothing.

It was however enough for Gandhi; in March he persuaded Congress to call off the mass campaign for a few petty concessions, and to participate in the Conference it had sworn to boycott. There were no commitments on self-government or home rule. Ordinances were to be withdrawn, and prisoners released – except those guilty of 'violence' or 'incitement to violence', or soldiers guilty of disobeying orders. This formula allowed Labour and Gandhi to exclude the Meerut detainees, a group of Sikh revolutionaries who were forthwith hanged, and 17 soldiers from the Garwhali Rifles, who were given severe sentences. With that, Gandhi was released to attend the Round Table Conference, a charade that continued for a year without resolution. As a contemporary Communist wrote:

'Hanging, flogging, slaying, shooting and bombing attest the efforts of parasitic imperialism to cling to the body of its victim. The Round Table Conference beside these efforts is like the ceremonial mumblings of the priest that walks behind the hangman.'[83]

There were sound reasons for Labour's intransigence. As *The Manchester Guardian* pointed out in 1930: 'There are two chief reasons why a self-regarding England may hesitate to relax her control over India. The first is that her influence in the past depends partly upon her power to summon troops and to draw resources from India in time of need . . . The second is that Great Britain finds in India her best market, and she has £1,000 million of capital invested there.'[84] The annual

---

82. *ibid*, p336.
83. R Page Arnot, *Labour Monthly*, September 1930, p534.
84. Quoted in R Palme Dutt, *ibid*, p497

tribute from India in the form of Home Charges, private remittances, and sterling indebtedness was currently of the order of £120–£150 million per annum. India absorbed 40 per cent of British cotton exports, which meant that the various Congress cotton boycotts had hit hard. That 'time of need' to which the *Guardian* referred occurred with the financial crisis of 1931, when $180 million worth of gold was plundered from India between October 1931 and March 1932 to bolster British imperialism. Well did *The Times* comment on 15 April 1930 that:

> 'Every farsighted view of our imperial interests, and of the hope of removing them altogether from party controversy, goes to show how important it is that a Labour government, and no other, should have the handling of the great external problems which are crowding upon us this year – the Naval Conference, the Imperial Conference, Egypt; above all, India.' [85]

A Naesmith, Secretary of the Weaver's Amalgamation, the largest textile union, echoed this view from the standpoint of the interests of the labour aristocracy when he told a mass meeting: 'they desired to see India and her people take their rightful place in the comity of nations, but not at the expense of the industrial and economic life of Lancashire and those dependent on it.' [86]

It had needed a Labour Government to re-establish British control over India. There is no more savage indictment of Labour than in its crushing of the Indian struggle of 1928–31, not even the crisis of 1931. Under a fog of democratic phrases, it acted savagely. It destroyed any chance of the Indian working class playing a significant role in the Indian liberation movement, which from thenceforward became the plaything of different bourgeois interests. In a debate in 1930, an ILP MP, WJ Brown, made a prophetic point when he told Parliament: 'I venture to suggest that we should regard it as a cardinal feature of

---

85. Quoted in R Page Arnot, *ibid*, p530.
86. Quoted in Gupta, *op cit*, p219.

British policy to carry Gandhi with us, for if we do not, we have to face the alternative to Gandhi, and that is organised violence and revolutionary effort.'[87] The reactionary nature of the neo-colonial solution of 1947 has its origins in this crucial phase of the struggle, when imperialism recognised that it would have to look to this bourgeois politician to safeguard its interests in an independent India.

2.11 The Middle East 1929-31

Labour policy in the Middle East picked up where it had left off five years earlier. With Egypt, continuity of policy with the previous Tory government was to be a hallmark; as Arthur Henderson, now Foreign Secretary explained, it had been 'a conspicuous part of the policy of each Government, including the Labour Government of 1924, to raise the relationship between Egypt and this country above party.'[88] This included incidents in both 1926 and 1927, when battleships had to be sent to Alexandria to remind the Egyptian government of the substance of this 'relationship', which had drawn no complaint from Labour. Henderson was again adamant about the need for British troops to remain in Suez – 'located there for the purpose of ensuring the defence of that vital artery of British Imperial communications'[89]; his attempt to force through a treaty legalising the de-facto British occupation failed as it had in 1924, without making the slightest difference to the substance of British policy.

Labour also needed to modify relations with Iraq in the face of nationalist rumblings; the 1924 Treaty was therefore re-negotiated with minor concessions: Britain was still left in control of foreign and military policy, was still to maintain its air bases, and could still occupy the country in the event of war – a power it was to use in 1941. Sidney Webb, now elevated to Lord Passfield, and Secretary of State for the Dominions and Colonies at the time, explained:

---

87. Quoted by Clemens Dutt, *Labour Monthly*, June 1930, p333.
88. Quoted in D Carlton, *MacDonald versus Henderson – The Foreign Policy of the Second Labour Government*, Macmillan, 1970, p164.
89. *ibid*.

'It may be asked, why do we want an alliance with Iraq at all? ... The answer to that question is, I think, that an alliance is vitally necessary in order to secure Imperial interests ... There is no other means of securing that unfettered use in all circumstances of our strategic air route, of adequately safeguarding our position at the head of the Persian Gulf.'[90]

In Palestine, a general strike during August 1929 by Palestinian workers and a revolt by the Arab peasantry against increasing Zionist expropriations was ruthlessly suppressed. 200 people were killed, mainly by British troops. On the direct orders of the Labour Government, nine Arab peasants were hanged, and several hundred more sentenced to long terms of imprisonment. Draconian legislation was passed which amongst other things made anti-imperialist agitation punishable by life imprisonment. A dispute between Lord Passfield and MacDonald over Jewish immigration, held to be at the root of the Palestinian uprising, was resolved in MacDonald's and the Zionists' favour to the extent that the apostle of Zionism, Chaim Weizmann, was to argue later that MacDonald's letter to him 'enabled us to make the magnificent gains of the ensuing years. It was under MacDonald's letter that Jewish immigration into Palestine was permitted to reach figures ... undreamed of in 1930'[91]

2.12 *Labour after 1931*

The second Labour Government fell in August 1931 following MacDonald's defection as a result of the crisis over public expenditure. In the autumn General Election, the Parliamentary Labour Party was reduced to an ineffectual rump of 52 MPs. The 1935 election brought a partial recovery (see below); politically, in imperial affairs, there was no wish to do other than maintain the bipartisan approach. One instance reflects this unchanging attitude: the response to the

90. Quoted in Gupta, *op cit*, p165.
91. Quoted in S Palmer, 'The Labour Party and Zionism', *Fight Racism! Fight Imperialism!* No 29, May 1983.

Palestinian rebellion in 1936, during the suppression of which over 1,000 people were killed. The British TUC, whose leaders, in particular Sir Walter Citrine and Ernest Bevin, dominated the Labour Party in this period, declared 'the Congress hopes that the British Government . . . will take all the necessary measures to bring the present disorders to an end.'[92] The Government certainly did: a further 5,000 Arabs were killed before the uprising was finally crushed three months later.

On foreign policy, there were occasional disagreements, but these were verbal in nature. For instance, Labour condemned the National Government when it refused to sanction action by the League of Nations against Italy after the latter's invasion of Abyssinia in 1935. Yet such opposition was confined to gestures: any working class move to boycott Italian goods was also roundly condemned. It was the same after the renewal of Japanese action against China in August 1937. Labour called for League of Nations action, in the full knowledge that the Government would not accept such a course of action; when dockers at Middlesborough and Southampton refused to handle Japanese goods, they were censured.

The craven nature of Labour was most evident in its response to the fascist insurrection in Spain in July 1936. British imperial policy was one of 'non-intervention', which by treating the Republican government and the fascist rebels as equals, gave tacit support for the latter. On 10 September, Citrine told the TUC Congress that non-intervention 'while on paper preventing the Fascist Powers from supplying munitions, was in fact being held up in such a way as to give those governments all the opportunities they needed for supplying arms . . . all the evidence proved you could not trust the word of Mussolini or Hitler'.[93] However he then went on to argue the case for non-intervention 'unpopular though it may be with large masses of our own people who do not understand perhaps the niceties of the question, because we believe that policy is right, however distasteful, and the

---

92. Quoted *ibid*.
93. Quoted in Miliband, *op cit*, p237.

policy which your wisdom will commend.'[94] A few days later at the Labour Party Conference, Arthur Greenwood, opening the debate on the subject, could only say that 'it was felt by all those who have considered this matter, sad though they were about it, that in the circumstances of the time, there was no alternative but this very, very second best of non-intervention.'[95] The policy was endorsed by a majority of over three to one.

Labour was formally to reverse this policy a year later; by this time, of course, it did not matter: the outcome had already been decided even if the war was to drag on another two years. Many were the international meetings of socialists, many were the pleas to governments to send arms to Republican Spain. Ruled out were any calls for action, Citrine making it plain that, in his view, industrial action would be illegal, and any joint action with the Communist Party completely unacceptable. All that remained was the ignominious acceptance that the Government would ignore their views anyway.

Labour expressed much concern about democracy when it saw its own interests imperilled, as in Spain; it would routinely denounce the 'dictatorial' nature of the Communist Party. However, democracy could never extend to the Empire, since that would also threaten its privileged position. Perhaps one of the most perceptive writers on Labour imperialism at this time was George Orwell. In an essay deliberately and provocatively entitled *Not Counting Niggers*, he argued that: 'above all in an imperialist country, left wing politics are always partly humbug', and criticised contemporary 'anti-fascism' because in proclaiming its defence of 'democracy' it ignored a 'far greater injustice' – the British Empire. He went on:

'What we always forget is that the overwhelming bulk of the British proletariat does not live in Britain but in Asia and Africa. It is not in Hitler's power, for instance, to make a penny an hour the

---

94. Quoted *ibid*, p238.
95. Quoted *ibid*, p239.

normal industrial wage; it is perfectly normal in India, and we are at great pains to keep it so.'[96]

To which might be added that the number of Indians who perished as a result of the famines that were a legacy of the British Raj were of the same order as those who died in the Nazi holocaust. Orwell was condemning those who were able to champion the superiority of British 'democracy' by conveniently forgetting to count the hundreds of millions of colonial slaves whose abject conditions made such a 'democracy' possible.

The outbreak of war gave Labour a new importance. The militarisation of labour would need the co-operation of the trade unions and the Labour Party; they were therefore drawn into the Churchill coalition of 1940. Labour's support for the coalition was to prove unconditional, despite the manner in which it prosecuted the war: securing British imperial interests first (the Middle East and the Mediterranean), before committing the resources necessary to defeat German fascism in mainland Europe. It also required very firm control of India, as it was to commit two million troops to Britain's war effort: it was also the last bastion against the westward drive of Japanese imperialism, and was critical to attempts to hold the Persian Gulf. Indian Congress support for the war was essential, and the Cabinet sent Stafford Cripps in March 1942 to negotiate with Gandhi. But Congress refused to accept any vague promise of self-government after the war, and initiated another campaign of civil disobedience. Once more, Congress and its associate organisations were banned and their leaders arrested, an act which occasioned protest only from Aneurin Bevan. On no issue involving colonial or foreign policy were there to be differences in substance between the two main partners of the coalition.

---

96. In ed S Orwell and I Angus, *The Collected Essays, Journalism and Letters of George Orwell*, vol 1, Penguin 1970, p437.

British Marines in action – Malaya 1950
(PHOTO: MARX MEMORIAL LIBRARY)

PART THREE

Labour and the reconstruction of the imperialist order 1945-51

3.1 *Britain's post-war crisis*

At the end of the Second World War imperialism faced a serious political crisis. The Allied powers had prosecuted the war under the slogans of democracy and national freedom, enshrining them in the Atlantic Charter. However, the enormous growth of national liberation movements in the colonial and semi-colonial countries showed that people throughout the world were not only taking such commitments seriously, but were organising to ensure they were put into effect. Many of these movements such as those in China, Malaya, Greece, Yugoslavia and Viet Nam were led by Communist Parties. In addition, a whole swathe of Eastern Europe was about to fall out of imperialist control, thereby strengthening the position of the Soviet Union. Meanwhile, much of Western Europe lay in ruins, its industry destroyed and its economies bankrupt.

If the overall position of imperialism was weak, that of British imperialism was precarious in the extreme. If it lost its colonial empire, post-war reconstruction would have to be undertaken at the direct expense of the British working class, with all the attendant risks of social upheaval. But it could not carry on in the old way: it had to offer the semblance of democratic concession to the colonial and semi-colonial peoples, if only to buy time. Of this the Tories were incapable:

Churchill's war-time declarations against Indian independence, his openly-declared refusal to preside over the dissolution of the Empire, would unleash the international forces that British imperialism most feared. Hence it turned to Labour, relying on its ability to dress up the defence of imperial interests in the language of democracy, socialism and the Atlantic Charter.

The problems presented to the incoming Labour Government were formidable. British imperialism was practically bankrupt in 1945. It had run up a huge external debt of £3,650 million, some 40 per cent of GNP. To finance its arms purchases from the USA, it had disposed of £1,000 million of overseas investment; the consequent fall in invisible income meant that it could no longer cover its huge visible trade deficit. Its dependency on US imperialism, the undisputed master of the capitalist world, became evident in December 1945 when the USA uni-laterally terminated the lend-lease scheme under which Britain had obtained favourable credit terms. Labour had to despatch a delegation to Washington to negotiate new credit, but at a market rate: the result was a loan of $3,750 million, which was obtained at the expense of a commitment to allow sterling holders to freely convert their pounds into dollars.

A fundamental issue was the trade imbalance between the two imperialist powers: over the next two years, British imports from the USA totalled £1,000 million whilst its exports in return were a paltry £180 million. The economic weakness of British imperialism therefore expressed itself in the form of dollar-indebtedness. To resolve it, and thereby escape economic dependency on the USA, Labour turned to the Empire; and despite the pressure to open it up to the USA:

' . . . the government exploited the colonies to the full. It required them to sell it their main export commodities at prices frequently well below world market levels. The government also accorded the colonies low priority for UK exports, preventing them from spending all their foreign exchange earnings. So the sterling balances grew in the late forties. Such high dollar earners as the Gold Coast [Ghana] and Malaysia were particularly ruthlessly

77

exploited, being forced to add their dollars to the Sterling Areas common pool, much of which was used to buy UK imports.'[1]

From 1948 in particular, the Empire was to be milked of all the dollars and superprofits it could earn. Resistance to this was to be ruthlessly and murderously put down. Three areas were to be critical: the Middle East, Malaya and West Africa. Such plunder was to cushion the British working class from the worst effects of the crisis, and help prevent a repetition of the revolutionary struggles that occurred after the First Imperialist War.

3.2   Greece [2]

The immediate issues at the end of the war for the Labour Government were the need to forestall revolution in South East Asia, safeguard the position within the Middle East, and prevent the spread of revolution within Europe itself. This last possibility was very real: partisan forces in Yugoslavia, Albania and Greece had effectively driven the German occupation forces out of their countries. Greece was of particular strategic importance because of its dominant position in the Eastern Mediterranean. The democratic movement had to be crushed if the approaches to the Middle East were to be safeguarded.

The intent was already clear when British troops landed in Greece in October 1944 and their commander, General Scobie, demanded that the Greek liberation force, EAM, and its armed wing, ELAS, both of which had overwhelming popular support, give up their arms. British imperialism's aim was to install a puppet government, supported by reactionary monarchist and quisling forces to guarantee its position. After a series of fascist attacks on ELAS supporters, EAM called a general strike in Athens on 4 December. Scobie promptly placed Athens under martial law and insisted that ELAS withdraw. Fighting

---

1. P Armstrong, A Glyn and J Harrison, *Capitalism since 1945*, Blackwell, 1991, pp61-62.
2. The material in this section, including all quotations, is drawn from R Clough, 'The Labour Party and Greece', *Fight Racism! Fight Imperialism!* No 36, February 1984.

broke out the following day; Churchill instructed Scobie to 'act as if you are in a conquered city where a local rebellion is in progress', and, later, 'the clear objective is the defeat of EAM. The ending of the fighting is subsidiary to this.'

Despite this blood-curdling threat, British forces were soon reduced to holding a few enclaves in Athens. Help was at hand from Labour, which was by happy chance holding its Conference at the same time. Ernest Bevin, who as a member of the Coalition Cabinet had been party to all its decisions, stated: 'The British Empire cannot abandon its position in the Mediterranean.' A motion condemning the British attack and calling for the withdrawal of British troops was overwhelmingly defeated, to be replaced by one calling on the Government 'to take all the necessary steps to facilitate an armistice without delay.' But the Government was doing just that, rushing in the reinforcements it needed to defeat ELAS. It took a force of 40,000 troops as well as RAF air support before it finally drove ELAS out of Athens in early February.

The following month saw fascist terror unleashed against EAM/ELAS under the direction of a British military occupation. By December 1945, 50,000 people had been prosecuted for EAM/ELAS activity, 18,000 were in gaol, and hundreds murdered, including Aris Velouchiotis, ELAS Supreme Commander. As Foreign Secretary in the new Labour Government, Bevin made it clear nothing was to change: 'His Majesty's Government adheres to the policy which they publicly supported when Greece was liberated.' Sir Walter Citrine, still TUC General Secretary, was sent to Greece in January 1945; thoughtfully provided with an interpreter whose Royalist father had been shot by ELAS for collaboration with the Nazis, he dutifully compiled a report informing the British labour movement of ELAS 'atrocities', referring to the Royalists' 'isolated acts of reprisals'.

As the terror continued, Labour ordered elections to be held in March 1946. Their own puppet 'liberal' prime minister complained about the fascist terror, an opinion dismissed by Bevin:

'I am much surprised by your statement that armed "X" [former collaborationist security forces] organisations will be reinforced by almost the whole of the police and gendarmeries. Such a statement is not borne out by the reports which I have received. In any case, I cannot see how "X" organisations can compel the electors in the countryside to vote in a manner contrary to their convictions, provided a secret ballot is secured.'

And this an election where women were not allowed to vote (although they had in EAM-liberated areas) and a quarter of the electoral register did not exist! No wonder a Greek opportunist socialist, who, unlike EAM, decided to participate in the elections, declared: 'We socialists in Greece are compromised by his [Bevin's] policy, as the people say to us: "If you are of Bevin's party, we cannot join you," and they turn more to the left.'

As the terror continued, ELAS re-grouped and started armed resistance from late 1946. The Royalist army, with British military backing, was unable to make any headway; by the beginning of 1947, the cost to Britain would approach £20 million per month. In February, Attlee told Truman that Britain could no longer afford the commitment, and would have to withdraw. British imperialism had forestalled the Greek revolution, but it could no longer be the lone policeman of the imperialist world. It would be left to the Americans to fund the final destruction of ELAS in 1949.

3.3   *South East Asia: Viet Nam* [3]

Whilst US imperialism took responsibility for forestalling revolution in North East Asia – in particular, China and Korea – Britain took responsibility for the South East – Viet Nam, Indonesia and Malaya. Following the defeat of Japan, insurrection swept Viet Nam under the leadership of the Viet Minh; revolutionary forces took over Hanoi on 19 August, Hue on 23 August, and Saigon two days later. On 2 September, a million people crowded into Hanoi's Ba Dinh Square to

---

3. Drawn from S Palmer, 'The Labour Party and Viet Nam' *Fight Racism! Fight Imperialism!*, No 31, August 1983.

hear Ho Chi Minh read a declaration of independence, and proclaim the Democratic Republic of Viet Nam (DRV).

On 11 September, an advance guard of over 20,000 British (in fact, overwhelmingly Indian) troops arrived in Saigon under the command of Major General Gracey. Under direction from the Labour Government, he refused to recognise the DRV, and gave the job of maintaining law and order to re-armed Japanese troops. A general strike on 17 September was met by a proclamation threatening summary execution for anybody taking part in a demonstration or public meeting or breaking the curfew. Next day, Gracey issued arms to French quisling colonial troops, who promptly organised a *coup d'état* with his blessing. With 40,000 Japanese troops at his disposal, Gracey started to clear the Viet Minh out of the major cities of the south, whilst French reinforcements were shipped in. In response to protests from Fenner Brockway, Prime Minister Attlee wrote 'the Government is carrying out the principles for which it has always stood', a fact that is uncontestable. Four days later, Bevin as Foreign Secretary had a meeting with the French Ambassador, and signed a secret agreement which guaranteed a British handover of Indochina in exchange for French withdrawal from Syria and Lebanon. In Parliament on 24 October, Bevin dishonestly claimed that the DRV was a Japanese creation, and confirmed that:

'every effort is being made to expedite the movement of French troops to Saigon in sufficient numbers to enable them to take over from the British forces.'

The British intervention was critical. The French were in no position to play a significant role in quelling the Viet Minh until early 1946. But for Labour, there would have been a revolutionary government in a united Viet Nam in 1945, not in 1975. The cost of Labour's restoration of the French can be measured in terms of 30 years' continuous war, millions of Viet Namese lives, and a ruined country.

3.4 *Indonesia*

A similar tale unfolded in Indonesia: of British intervention to restore a colonial power, and of secret agreements to support such intervention.

It started on 15 August, when the Japanese surrendered to the Indonesian National Liberation forces, which then established a provisional government with Soekarno as President. On 15 September, the first British troops landed in Java under General Christison, who announced: 'We are not going to put the Dutch back in power.' But with him came instructions that the Japanese army was to help restore the *status quo* and repress any disturbances, together with further orders banning all popular assemblies, the raising of the new national flag, and the carrying of arms. During September, Australian troops under overall British command were able to occupy Borneo and Sulavesi with little resistance, since the liberation forces were relatively weak on these two islands, and thus start the process of restoring the Dutch colonial administration.

At the same time, British reinforcements landed on Java, whilst Japanese forces took control of the major towns of Badang and Samarang in Sumatra in anticipation of a British invasion. On 25 October, British troops landed at Surabaya, preceded by a small Dutch party, which was promptly detained by the Indonesian republic. Two weeks later, in an effort to buy time, the Dutch made an 'offer' to the provisional Indonesian government: provided it disarmed, ended the republic and recognised Dutch rule, there would be a 'reconstruction' of the colonial government at some time in the future involving directly elected representatives, on a suffrage subject to further discussion. Noel–Baker, Labour Minister of State at the Foreign Office, described the suggested surrender as 'generous and far-reaching'; not surprisingly, the Indonesians themselves rejected it out of hand. Two weeks later, Bevin declared in the House of Commons:

'It is clear that HM Government have a definite agreement with [the Dutch] to provide for the Dutch East Indies Government to resume as rapidly as practicable full responsibility for the administration of the Netherlands Indian Territories.'[4]

This was the first indication that there had been a secret agreement with the Dutch to restore colonial rule in Indonesia, an agreement which had in fact been concluded as early as 24 August. Its full import became apparent at Surabaya, a stronghold of the liberation movement. In an attempt to force the republic to give up its Dutch captives, the RAF dropped leaflets on 9 November demanding the unconditional surrender of its leaders together with its arms. The following day, the city was shelled by 25-pounders, by a cruiser and four destroyers, and bombed by the RAF. Using tanks and armoured cars against youths armed with rifles, bows and arrows and machetes, the British took four weeks to capture the city, with the assistance of re-armed Japanese soldiers, an achievement which was then repeated at Bandung. By the time British troops withdrew in November 1946, they had inflicted 40,000 casualties, and left Dutch imperialism to impose a favourable neo-colonial solution.

3.5   *The Middle East*

Control of the Middle East was a crucial plank in Labour's foreign policy. Its aim was to restore as much of the status quo before the war as possible – in other words, retain control of the Suez Canal, and sustain the string of puppet regimes through which British imperialism had controlled the oil reserves of the region since 1918.

After the unsuccessful efforts of Labour in 1924 and 1929, British imperialism had imposed a treaty on Egypt in 1936: its terms formalised British control of Egyptian foreign and military policy, and allowed 10,000 British troops to be stationed in Suez for the next 20 years, that is until 1956. But by March 1946, mass demonstrations were demanding its abrogation. Labour was not to be moved: it would not withdraw troops unless the Egyptian government were to sign a

---

4. Quoted in A Clegg, *Hands Off Indonesia*, CPGB, 1946, p12.

'mutual defence' pact which would allow Britain unfettered use of the Canal, and it would not concede Egyptian demands for federation with Sudan. In January 1947, Labour broke off negotiations, retaining 80,000 troops in the Suez bases for the remainder of its term of office.

No long-term solution was possible in Iraq either: the awakening of nationalist opinion required re-negotiation of the 1930 Treaty. Labour was determined to ensure that even if it had to relinquish direct control of the Iraqi government, it should retain its RAF bases to assure control of Iranian as well as Iraqi oil. The Treaty was signed in Portsmouth in 1948; the immediate response was a near-insurrection in Baghdad, which forced the puppet regime to reject it. Once again, stalemate resulted: the Treaty was put into effect even if it was not accepted; however, Britain's position had been fatally weakened, and it was to be expelled within ten years.

The most serious debacle was in Palestine. The 1944 Labour Conference, as well as supporting intervention in Greece, took a rabidly pro-Zionist standpoint: 'Let the Arabs be encouraged to move out as the Jews move in. Let them be compensated handsomely for their land and let their settlement elsewhere be carefully organised and generously financed ... Indeed, we should re-examine the possibility of extending the present Palestinian boundaries, by agreement with Egypt, Syria or Jordan.' Even Chaim Weizmann was alarmed that Labour 'in their pro-Zionist enthusiasm, went far beyond our intentions.'[5]

However, in power, Bevin and Labour were more concerned about alliances with puppet Arab regimes than with Zionist demands for the partition of Palestine. Bevin was opposed by the Labour left, led by Bevan and Foot (whose support for Zionism was expressed in racist contempt for the Arab people) who argued that a Zionist state would prove a more stable bulwark against the Soviet Union. The Zionists responded with a terror campaign directed against Palestinians and British troops alike. They were comforted in the knowledge that they were backed by US imperialism, which saw in the conflict the lever with which it could evict British imperialism from its predominant role

5. Quoted in S Palmer, *op cit.*

in the region. Labour announced it would withdraw troops from Palestine in May 1948; by carefully re-inforcing the TransJordanian army, it hoped that in a war with its Arab neighbours, the Zionist forces would be humiliated. The subsequent military fiasco proved Labour's calculations wrong, and the legacy is with the Palestinian people today.

3.6   *India*

The 1945 Labour Election Manifesto, *Let us Face the Future*, had said nothing about the colonies except that in relationship to India it was prepared to offer self-government. However, Congress leaders, who had spent most of the war in gaol, were in no position to accept this: there were widespread mutinies amongst Indian troops, and a full-scale revolt in the Navy in February 1946. The Indian people had few enough illusions in Labour: Cripps, who was still outside the Party in 1942 having been expelled in the 1930s, was now back in, and many remembered that he had endorsed suppression of Congress after the failure of his mission in 1942.

Imperialist policy had been to encourage the formation of a bourgeois Muslim movement as a counter-weight to the mainly Hindu, but equally bourgeois, Congress. There were real material differences between the two bourgeoisies, but the suppression of Congress during the war had given space to the Moslem League to mobilise the bulk of the Moslem population behind a plan for a state independent of India. The consequences of the Meerut trial were now evident: only the working class movement in the vanguard of the oppressed could have prevented the disintegration of the liberation struggle into a factional struggle between competing bourgeois interests. Despite this, there was no chance for British imperialism to re-assert its pre-war position, and in March 1947, Labour appointed Lord Mountbatten as Viceroy of India, with a commitment to bring about a British withdrawal by June 1948.

Even this timetable proved optimistic, for within three months the date for withdrawal was advanced to August 1947, as India proved completely ungovernable: Attlee himself was to concede 'No doubt we could have held India for two or three years longer. But we could have done so only at the cost of a great expenditure of men and money.'[6] Such men, being Indian, would have been at best unreliable and, given the precarious financial state of British imperialism, the money was not there to finance them anyway. Lord Ismay, Mountbatten's Chief of Staff, was more blunt: 'India in March 1947 was a ship on fire in mid-ocean with ammunition in the hold. By then it was a question of putting out the fire before it reached the ammunition. There was, in fact, no option before us but to do what we did.'[7] Labour conceded independence, not because it had wanted to, but because there was no other way. Hundreds of thousands were to die in a series of communal massacres as the Moslem and Hindu ruling classes staked their territorial claims. India and Pakistan had been saved for imperialism.

3.7   Oil and Iran

British oil interests in the Middle East after the war were still enormous: Anglo Iranian Oil Company (AIOC) controlled all Iranian oil output, and owned the biggest oil refinery in the world at Abadan, a capital asset of £350 million. It owned 25 per cent of the Iraq Petroleum Company (with Shell holding a further 25 per cent), and 50 per cent of the Kuwaiti Oil Company (Shell again effectively holding 25 per cent through an agreement with Gulf), and overall directly controlled 58 per cent of Middle East oil reserves against the US's 35 per cent. The average cost of producing Middle East oil at this time was around $0.10 per barrel, compared with $0.50 in Venezuela, at that time the largest oil-exporter, and $1.10 in the USA. But through their monopoly control of the world's oil, the seven US and British oil giants set the price of oil to ensure the profitability of domestic US production. Fabulous profits could be made in the Middle East. As post-war oil production boomed to meet increasing demand, so did the profits of AIOC (Table 5).

---

6. Quoted in B Moore, *Labour-Communist Relations 1920-51*, Part 3, Our History Pamphlet 84/85, CPGB, 1991, p15.
7. Quoted in Palme Dutt, *op cit*, p191.

Table 5   **Iranian Oil Revenues 1946-50** [8]

Year	Iranian Oil Production (million tons)	AIOC Net Profits (£000s)	AIOC British Tax Payments (£000s)	AIOC Royalty Payments (£000s)
1946	19.2	9,625	10,279	7,132
1947	20.2	18,565	15,266	7,104
1948	24.9	24,065	28,310	9,172
1949	26.8	18,390	22,480	13,489
1950	31.8	33,103	50,707	16,032

Total declared remittances to Britain came to some £54 million in 1946-7, and climbed to £177 million over the next three years, when royalty payments to Iran came to less than £40 million. Even this is an under-estimate: gross profits in 1950 were £147 million. The Iranian government received little more than 10 per cent of this total. Not for nothing had Bevin declared of the Middle East:

> 'His Majesty's Government must maintain a continuing interest in that area if only because our economic and financial interests in the Middle East are of vast importance to us . . . If these interests were lost to us, the effect on the life of this country would be a considerable reduction in the standard of living . . . British interests in the Middle East contribute substantially not only to the interests of the people there, but to the wage packets of the workpeople of this country.'[9]

Incensed by the nakedness of this plunder, the Iranian people forced the Mossadeq government to nationalise AIOC in 1951. The response of Labour was immediate: it despatched a cruiser and destroyers to Abadan and imposed a world-wide oil embargo on Iran; only its weakened

8. From Z Mikdashi, *A Financial Analysis of Middle East Oil Concessions 1901-65*, Praeger, 1966, p110.
9. Quoted in R Palme Dutt, *The Crisis of Britain and the British Empire*, Lawrence and Wishart, 1954, pp336-37.

military status prevented it going to war. It was left to the incoming Tory Government to conclude the matter by organising a coup with the CIA which destroyed Mossadeq and brought Iran and its oil back under imperialist control – with Britain retaining only a minority stake.

British control of Iranian oil was not only vastly profitable in the years to 1951, it also avoided expenditure of dollars. However, if AIOC was brazen about its profitability, its larger cousin by a factor of four, Royal Dutch Shell, was far more secretive. Shell's holdings lay traditionally in Dutch East Indies and Latin America, but its increasing Middle East interests also boosted profitability to a level which dwarfed AIOC: gross profits were £190 million in 1950 and no less than £249 million in 1951, which at about 2 per cent of British GNP would be equivalent to more than £10 billion today.

Bevin understood very well the nature of imperialist parasitism.

3.8 Malaya: rubber and tin

Through its occupation of Malaya, Britain controlled the source of 45 per cent of the world's natural rubber, and 30 per cent of the world's output of tin. It monopolised a natural resource which was vital to US imperialism, since most of the remainder of the world's rubber and tin reserves lay in Indonesia. 'Plunder' does not even begin to describe how this was used to bolster Britain's financial position.

From 1946 to 1951, total British exports to the US amounted to £515 million. Over the same period, total Malayan exports to the US came to £460 million. In 1950, when British exports to the US came to £127.3 million, Malayan exports came to £122 million; in 1951, the respective figures were £154.7 million and £166 million. A US Mission despatched to Malaya in 1950 noted the high rate of return on British investment in Malaya and stated:

> '[Malayan] exports to the US were valued at $215,426,831 in 1948 and $182,809,000 in 1949. The area is the largest net dollar earner in the whole sterling area. Malaya's exports, especially of rubber and tin, to dollar markets are of critical importance in the effort to

achieve a balance of payments between the sterling and dollar areas. Without these dollar earnings, the UK would... face a noticeable reduction in its already austere standard of living.'[10]

Workers in Malaya bore the full brunt of Labour's need for dollars, and in particular the Indian and Chinese labourers who had been imported to work the plantations and mines. Between 1939 and 1949, their real wages fell by nearly 80 per cent, while the plantation own-ers announced record dividends. Whilst the Labour Government attempted to forge a racist constitution which would guarantee a privileged position to the feudal sultans on the one hand and the indigenous middle class Malayans on the other, the national liberation forces succeeded in building a trade union movement, the Pan Malayan Federation of Trade Unions (PMFTU), which united all workers. Labour's hostility was undisguised: 'The parliamentary Under-Secretary of State for Colonies, Ivor Thomas, became concerned after a visit to Malaya in February 1947, to ensure the unimpeded production of rubber, "a dollar earning commodity". He also shared the anti-Chinese and pro-Malay bias of Gent [Governor of Malaya], blamed the estate workers for strikes and frequent wage demands and recom-mended flogging and banishment as punishment for breaches of law and order.'[11]

Working class resistance was met with brutality; workers were regularly gunned down by police; in April and May 1948, eight workers were killed; on 1 June, seven plantation workers were beaten to death for refusing to end an estate occupation. 12 days later, the government banned the PMFTU, and arrested hundreds of its leaders. In May 1949, its former President, SA Ganapathy, was hanged for alleged possession of a gun, to be followed the next day by the former Vice-President, Veerasenam. The destruction of the trade union movement left the Malayan Communist Party (MCP) no option but to resort to

---

10. Quoted in M Caldwell, in ed M Amin and M Caldwell, *Malaya – The Making of a Neo-Colony*, p248.
11. PS Gupta, in ed J Winter, *The Working Class in Modern British History*, Cambridge, 1983, p114.

armed struggle, a struggle that was to last in all for 12 years before it was finally defeated. The Labour Government rushed huge forces to Malaya to deal with what it referred to with racist contempt as the 'bandits'. It set up concentration camps, put prices on the heads of known MCP leaders, used assassination squads, and even unleashed Dyak head-hunters to terrorise the nationalist population. After all, as the then Tribunite Woodrow Wyatt asked: 'What would happen to our balance of payments if we had to take our troops out of Malaya?'[12]

3.9 West Africa: cocoa and vegetable oil

The two major West African colonies – Nigeria and the Gold Coast – were sources of cocoa, and palm nut and groundnut oil. During the War, British imperialism had set up a system of Marketing Boards in these colonies to act as monopoly purchasers of the cash crops grown by African farmers. The Boards would buy the complete annual crop, ship it to Britain, and then re-sell it on the world – or, rather, the US market. In 1947, therefore, the Gold Coast Cocoa Marketing Board bought the entire cocoa crop at £67 per ton in sterling, and re-sold it all in London in dollars to the US chocolate manufacturers at £177 per ton. This netted the British Government £16 million in 1947, and together with the Nigerian cocoa crop £38 million in 1948. By simultaneously holding down imports into these colonies, British imperialism was able to build up a huge surplus on their trade (Table 6), and convert them into forced loans in the form of sterling balances.

The net surplus from 1948-51 from these two colonies came to over £190 million. The plunder was naked: in 1946-7 the West Africa Produce Board bought palm oil from farmers at £16.15s per ton and resold it in London at £95 per ton; in the same year, groundnuts were bought at £15 per ton, whilst their oil was realising £110 per ton. The power that British imperialism had given itself as a monopoly purchaser in 1939 served it well in the post-war years: ' . . . a system of bulk

---

12. Quoted in R Palme Dutt, *ibid*, p104.

Table 6   **Trade surplus of Gold Coast [Ghana] and Nigeria 1946-51 (£000s)** [13]

Year	Nigeria			Gold Coast		
	Imports	Exports	Balance	Imports	Exports	Balance
1946	19,824	24,626	+ 4,802	13,220	20,303	+ 7,083
1948	41,947	62,741	+20,524	31,378	56,115	+24,737
1949	58,231	81,067	+22,836	45,416	49,927	+ 4,511
1950	61,866	90,168	+28,302	48,129	77,407	+29,278
1951	84,554	120,064	+35,510	63,793	91,900	+28,197

buying, which began life as a wartime device, was prolonged after 1945 as part of Labour's system of tapping colonial resources.' [14]

No wonder Stafford Cripps, the Chancellor of the Exchequer, had argued during the acute crisis of November 1947 that 'the whole future of the sterling group and its ability to survive depend, in my view, upon a quick and extensive development of our African resources.' He went on to argue at a conference of African governors:

'You will, I understand, be considering the question of the development of manufactories and industries in the colonies. Though I take the view that such development is highly desirable so long as it is not pushed too far or too quickly, yet it must be obvious that with the present world shortage of capital goods, it is not possible to contemplate much in the way of industrial development of the colonies.' [15]

His conclusion?

'Our desperate need in the next few years is, first, to find ways of increasing our capital resources available for investment, and,

---

13. Drawn from R Ekundare, *An Economic History of Nigeria 1860-1960*, Methuen, 1973, p412; also, ed GB Kay, *The Political Economy of Colonialism in Ghana*, Cambridge, 1972, p326.
14. DK Fieldhouse in R Ovendale, *The Foreign Policy of the British Labour Governments 1945-51*, Leicester, 1984, p97.
15. Quoted in R Palme Dutt, *ibid*, p248.

secondly, to invest that capital in the most profitable way so as to bring in quick results. The colonies can make their contribution to the first need by reducing demands for unnecessary current consumption and devoting some of their own earnings to capital purposes.'[16]

This view was echoed by the former 'extreme' leftist John Strachey, by now a far more 'realistic' Minister of Food:

'By hook or by crook the development of primary production of all sorts in the colonial territories and dependent areas in the Commonwealth and throughout the world is a life and death matter for the economy of this country.'[17]

The infamous Tanganyika groundnuts scheme was precisely the sort of project Labour had in mind. Initiated by the Chairman of the United Africa Company (UAC), a Unilever subsidiary, it proposed the development of vast groundnut plantations in Tanganyika, to supplement those in West Africa, where UAC already held a monopoly. So enthusiastic was the Government as to its prospects – it estimated an annual dollar saving of £10 million – that it increased the size of the initial project by 50 per cent, bringing the total acreage to 3.25 million, or some 5,000 square miles. At the end of 1946, the Treasury advanced £25 million to the UAC to commence clearing operations. However, Tanganyika was not a British colony, but an ex-German territory which Britain held now as a UN Mandate. Under the terms of the mandate, Britain was obliged to consult the UN before undertaking such a development. However, Labour was in too much of a hurry for such niceties, so, 'without consulting the Trusteeship Council of the UN, on whose behalf the Labour Government is supposed to hold the territory in trust until the Africans are able to take over the administration, Mr Creech Jones agreed to alienate some 3,250,000 acres of native land and hand it over to the Ministry of Food at an annual

---

16. Quoted in G Padmore, *Africa – Britain's Third Empire*, Dobson, 1948, p190.
17. Quoted in R Palme Dutt, *op cit*, p249.

rental of five cents an acre.'[18]. In March 1949, John Strachey was already revelling in the possibilities:

> 'If the British Empire does not flourish, the sovereignty over those areas which is at present held by this House will be lost to the House because the one thing that will not happen is that these areas will be left barren and undeveloped. If we do not do the job, some other Power or persons will, because the world cannot tolerate that this vast land should be left in the state in which it has too long lingered . . . I have the perfect confidence that in a very few years the groundnut scheme will be one of the acknowledged glories of the British Commonwealth.'[19]

Too soon, however, for later that year, after the expenditure of £23 million, only 26,000 acres had been brought under cultivation owing to the difficulties of clearing the land; even worse, the yield was less than the seed used. The scheme was reduced in scope first to 600,000 acres, and then to 200,000. Defending it just before it was abandoned as a complete fiasco with a loss of £36 million, Strachey said:

> 'The scheme is a thoroughly hard-headed and not philanthropic proposition . . . painful readjustments for the African population . . . this is not a philanthropic scheme started purely and solely for the African's benefit.'[20]

Quite. In 1948, the then Governor of Tanganyika had explained clearly what he thought was of benefit to the African population when he defended the practice of flogging as 'a suitable punishment' before the UN Trusteeship Council on the grounds that 'imprisonment was not

---

18. Quoted in G Padmore, *op cit*, p176. Creech Jones' position contrasts with what he had argued in *Tribune* in 1944 in an article on the Cameroons. His view then was that 'Trusteeship is cant and humbug unless it is implemented in constructive terms of development and social targets, and unless that development is for and in the interests of the African people.' (Quoted *ibid*, p187).

19. Quoted in Amanke Okafor, *Nigeria – Why we Fight For Independence*, 1950, p26.

20. Quoted in R Palme Dutt, *op cit*, p250.

understood, since in prison the African would be better off than at home.'[21]

3.10   *Sterling balances and overseas investment*

The massive trade surplus of the colonies did not just mean superprofits for the companies involved, let alone dollars for the British Empire. Labour was able to use Britain's financial control of its colonies to retain part of the payments for the colonies' exports as a loan whose rate of interest and date of repayment were determined by British imperialism. These credits were originally a method of pooling the hard currency earnings of the colonies to pay for US goods during the war; Britain bought such hard currency at the rate of exchange it chose to establish, and in return credited the colonies with an appropriate sterling balance. These balances had increased enormously during the war; those credited to India alone rising by £1,300 million between 1939 and 1946, even though it was nominally a Dominion. Things did not change with the end of the war; in fact, the sterling balances of the colonies continued to rise as those of the Dominions fell. As Palme Dutt observed:

'This post-war increase in the colonial sterling balances represents a further volume of goods drawn from the colonial countries, and used in practice to meet Britain's dollar deficit, without any current payment to the colonial peoples other than a depreciating and irredeemable paper credit in London....The increase in the colonial balances is a measure of the increase in the special intensified exploitation of the colonial peoples during these years, additional to the "normal" flow of colonial tribute.'[22]

A condition of the 1945 US loan was that these sterling balances become freely convertible into dollars a year from the date the loan was finally approved. When that date, July 1946, arrived, a huge run on the

---

21. Quoted in A Medora and J Woddis, *Social Security in the Colonies*, World Federation of Trade Unions, circa 1952, p47.
22. Quoted in R Palme Dutt, *op cit*, pp266-67

Table 7   **Sterling balances 1945-51**   (£000,000s) [23]

UK Sterling Debts to:	1945	1948	1951	Increase Total	%
Sterling Area:					
Colonies	446	556	964	+518	+116
Other Sterling Areas	2007	1809	1825	−182	−9
Non-Sterling Area	3663	3701	3807	−192	−16

pound started; by mid–September most of the loan had been used trying to defend the sterling area. Convertibility had to be suspended, since British imperialism had proved too weak to survive without the enforced financial support of the Empire. When in 1949 Labour finally devalued the pound, its control of colonial currency allowed it to maintain a fixed exchange rate with the metropolitan currency, with the result that 'the British, while having to devalue the pound against the dollar . . . kept the pound strong against all colonial currencies (in most cases at par) by devaluing them at the same time and to the same extent. In short, the sterling area was used after 1945 as a device for supporting the pound sterling against the dollar long after it had lost its legitimate function of pooling Empire and Commonwealth resources for the fight against fascism. At the same time the pound was kept strong against the colonial currencies to avoid an increase in the real burden of blocked sterling balances. In both ways, the colonies were compelled to subsidise Britain's post–war standard of living.' [24]

The increase in these forced loans co-incided with a huge increase in overseas investment by British imperialism – a total of £659 million between 1948 and the first half of 1951 alone. Hugh Dalton, Chancellor of the Exchequer before Cripps, described the relationship between Britain and the colonies in the form of a fictional conversation with an Indian:

---

23. *ibid.*
24. DK Fieldhouse, in R Ovendale, *op cit*, p96.

'For years you have been in debt to us, and you have paid up: our political control of you ensured that. Now the wheel of fortune has turned full circle: we are indebted to you. It is true that you are poor and we are rich, and that you need our funds for your economic development. But I am afraid we are not going to pay up.'[25]

Fieldhouse has argued that the period of post-war shortages and the Korean commodity boom represented the best conditions for the impoverished colonies to begin to create an infrastructure which would allow for a substantial economic development. However, 'these opportunities were lost because the Labour Government used the colonies to protect the British consumer from the high social price which continental countries were then paying for their post-war reconstruction. Consciously or not, this was to adopt "social imperialism" in an extreme form.'[26] Oliver Lyttleton, shortly to become Tory Colonial Secretary, commented pointedly during the October 1951 Election campaign that: 'The Government claims that the dependent territories were exploited in the past, but are not being exploited now. But in fact, the Socialist Government seems to be the first government which has discovered how to exploit the colonies.'[27]

3.11   The African Empire

Since its 1917 response to the Bolshevik peace proposals, Labour had not changed its stance on the African colonies. Creech Jones wrote in 1944, two years before he was to become Colonial Secretary: 'Socialists . . . cannot stop their ears to the claims of the colonial people and renounce responsibility towards British territories because of some sentimental inclination to "liberation" or internal administration. To

---

25. Quoted in DN Pritt, *The Labour Government 1945-51*, Lawrence and Wishart 1963, p136.
26. In R Ovendale, *op cit*, p99.
27. Quoted in R Palme Dutt, *ibid*, p270.

throw off the colonial empire in this way, would be to betray the peoples and our trust.'[28] In line with this reasoning, not one African colony received independence from the Labour Government, as it took literally its 1943 policy document that 'the inhabitants of the African territories are "backward" and "not yet able to stand by themselves" ', and opposed any reference to the Atlantic Charter because it mentioned self-government.[29]

The 'responsibility' with which Creech Jones was so concerned became evident during the Seretse Khama affair. Seretse Khama was heir to the chiefdom of Bechuanaland, a British protectorate bordering on South Africa. When he was formally elected chief by a huge majority, the apartheid regime protested because he had had the temerity to marry a white woman, and demanded his removal. In March 1950, Labour banished him from his homeland to maintain favour with South Africa, which had become an important ally, both economically and strategically. Hence early in 1948, Harold Wilson, as President of the Board of Trade, had singled it out 'as one market of particular importance in view of its position as an important gold producer. Exports to this market may indeed not only save dollars but earn us gold',[30] whilst Dalton as the Chancellor of Exchequer had found South Africa 'particularly helpful' during the sterling crisis of 1947. From 1946 to 1955, British investments were to total some £500 million. Nor was it just the economic significance: there was the Simonstown naval base, and perhaps most importantly of all, uranium – in fact the only uranium source outside US or Soviet control. With Labour now secretly committed to the development of a British A-bomb, there was not the slightest chance it would jeopardise its relationship with apartheid by a dispute over the chieftanship of an 'insignificant' colony.

The Seretse Khama affair was one in a series of episodes which displayed an underlying sympathy with minority settler regimes.

28. Quoted *ibid*, p335.
29. Quoted in Gupta, *op cit*, p276.
30. Quoted in P Foot, *The Politics of Harold Wilson*, Penguin, 1968, p270.

Already, in 1946, Labour had conceded the mandate over the former German colony South West Africa (Namibia) to South Africa, and later supported the apartheid regime in its resistance to giving up control to the United Nations, arguing that South Africa had a perfect right to retain the ex-colony. A White Paper in March 1947 granted an unofficial majority to white settlers in Kenya in the legislature, based on communal representation. When in the following year the Kenyan African Union (KAU) adopted a democratic programme, Creech Jones commented that: 'democratic government in the hands of ignorant and politically inexperienced people can easily become unworkable'.[31] Two years later, the Communist-led East African TUC called a boycott of a visit by the Queen: the boycott itself was declared illegal, and when its leaders were detained, the response was an 18-day general strike. Labour rushed in troops, arrested hundreds of workers and banned the union. In December 1950, the new Colonial Secretary, James Griffiths, conceded the possibility of future self-government for Kenya, but by failing to state that it would be based on one person one vote, in fact accepted settler demands for parity with other races.

The other demonstration of pro-settler sympathy came with the proposal for a Central African Federation, which would include Southern Rhodesia (Zimbabwe), Northern Rhodesia (Zambia) and Nyasaland (Malawi). Again, nuclear technology was a prime consideration for British imperialism: Southern Rhodesia was a crucial sterling area source of chromium. The federation would of course be dominated by the tiny settler populations; for Labour, this was not an obstacle, neither were the unanimous objections of the African population led by the likes of Hastings Banda. By the time Labour left office, it had sanctioned Federation, with Griffiths an enthusiastic supporter.

Such sympathy was not to be dispensed when Africans insisted that they were more than capable of self-determination. When the influential Fabian Colonial Bureau (Creech Jones was its effective spokes-

---

31. Quoted in E Abrahams, 'The Labour Party and Kenya', *Fight Racism! Fight Imperialism!* No 32, September 1983.

man) organised a conference in January 1946, inviting various colonial representatives, Rita Hinden, its secretary, clashed with Kwame Nkrumah:

> 'When Mr Nkrumah said "we want absolute independence" it left me absolutely cool. Why? . . . British socialists are not so concerned with ideals like independence and self-government, but with the idea of social justice. When British socialists look at the Eastern Europe of today they ask themselves whether independence is itself a worthwhile aim.'[32]

From its tiny population of three million, the Gold Coast had provided 70,000 servicemen for the imperialist war effort. The response was a 1947 constitution where the appointed Governor had an absolute veto over a legislative council, two-fifths of which was made up of appointees. On 28 February 1948, police fired on a demonstration of demobilised servicemen protesting against the rising cost of living. Two were killed; there was a massive uprising in response. A split appeared in the existing bourgeois freedom movement, the United Gold Coast Convention (UGCC), one wing under Joseph Danquah attempting to restrain the struggle and compromise, the other, under Nkrumah's leadership, adopting a programme of social reform and immediate self-government. Creech-Jones attempted to exclude Nkrumah from the political scene by making concessions to Danquah: 'The Gold Coast is on the edge of revolution. We are in danger of losing it', he told the Governor of the colony.[33] Faced with such manoeuvring, the mass of the people forced an open split, and at a 60,000-strong meeting in June 1949, Nkrumah split with the mass of the UGCC membership to form the Convention People's Party (CPP).

In October 1949, a revised constitution was presented, making no significant concessions other than to the lawyer-merchant class led by Danquah; its terms of reference had specifically excluded any consider-

---

32. Quoted in Gupta, *Imperialism and the British Labour Movement, op cit*, p326.
33. Quoted in B Lapping, *End of Empire*, Guild Publishing, 1985, p373.

ation of self-government. On 20 November, a representative constituent assembly of 500 organisations including the trade unions demanded immediate dominion status, and proposed amendments to the constitution to frame this. The demand was immediately rejected by the Colonial Secretary, and a civil disobedience campaign started. The Gold Coast TUC called a general strike on 8 January 1950; the Governor declared a state of siege; Nkrumah along with other CPP and Gold Coast TUC leaders, was arrested. However, as a tactical move, the CPP decided to contest elections to be held under the new constitution, and obtained a landslide victory. Labour had to backtrack and release Nkrumah lest events moved completely out of control. The Gold Coast thus became the only African colony to make significant progress towards independence, and the biggest obstacle it had faced was the Labour Government's determination to maintain direct control of its dollar-earning capacity.

3.12   *NATO and the Soviet Union*

Labour could not rebuild the world imperialist order on its own. There might be some with delusions that Britain was still a great power on a par with the USA, but the latter's economic might was overwhelming, and could be expressed in a myriad of ways – from the termination of Lend-Lease to its refusal to share atomic secrets with Britain. But the initial confrontations with the Soviet Union were led by Britain as it tried to reclaim its empire. Indeed, there were a number of sharp disagreements in the aftermath of the war where the USA, anxious to break up the old European empires, seemed to some to be too close to the Soviet Union: US observers in Viet Nam were opposed to the British actions; there were also disagreements over the British role in Greece and Indonesia, not to mention over Zionist claims to Palestine.

The first serious disagreements between Britain and the Soviet Union took place within a couple of months of the end of the war: they concerned British plans for the former Italian colonies in Africa (Somalia and Cyrenaica, the latter now part of Libya), its designs on Persia (now Iran), the British role in South East Asia, and shortly afterwards Germany. In Persia, Soviet backing for an Azeri republic in the north of the country was faced down by Britain, and Soviet troops withdrew in May 1946: 'Iran settled down again into its traditional client role of indirect tutelage, an intrinsic element in Britain's economic and strategic "lifeline" as proclaimed by Bevin.'[34]

It was in fact early 1946 when US policy seemed to swing definitively behind Labour's in isolating the Soviet Union. It supported Britain in Persia and started to play a more active role in the rebuilding of capitalist Europe. It was also getting increasingly involved in the civil war in China; in the four years from 1945 it spent over $3 billion in economic and military aid in bolstering the reactionary Chiang Kai Shek against the Communist-led liberation struggle. The point at which it definitely took over the leadership of the imperialist alliance from Britain was in March 1947, when Labour announced that it could not defeat the Greek revolutionary movement and would have to withdraw its forces. US President Truman declared 'that it must be the policy of the United States to support free peoples who are resisting attempted subjugation by armed minorities or by outside pressure.' Truman's announcement was followed by the immediate despatch of economic and military aid to both Greece and Turkey. In short order there followed the eviction of the Communist Parties from both the Italian and French governments, and the establishment of the Marshall Plan to promote European reconstruction.

The military corollary of this process was the establishment of NATO in 1949, in which Bevin played the leading role. NATO was set up to contain the Soviet Union, not because it might march through Western Europe, but rather to isolate it from the growing anti-colonial movement which was now in the vanguard of the revolutionary struggle. In other words, NATO was a thinly-veiled warning to the Soviet Union to either drop or severely curtail any support for national liberation struggles. The Labour left was an enthusiastic supporter of such intimidation: *Tribune* was writing regularly about the dangers of

---

34. KO Morgan, *Labour in Power 1945-51*, Oxford, 1985, p251.

appeasement, and had applauded the 1948 re-election of Truman to the White House. Thus there was never any question of Labour's commitment to NATO from the outset: even when it adopted a policy of unilateral disarmament in the early 1980s, it never dropped its allegiance to the imperialist alliance.

3.13   The Korean War

The final shame of the Labour Government was its support for the neo-fascist Syngman Rhee regime in South Korea. In August 1945, Korea had been partitioned along the 38th Parallel. In the North, the regime, made up of veterans of the war against the Japanese occupation of both Korea and Manchuria, had instituted a widespread land reform, and purged the state apparatus of those who had collaborated with the Japanese colonialists. In the South, under the direction of the US, quite the opposite had happened: there was no land reform, and the regime was controlled by former stooges of the Japanese occupation. The political stability of the regime in the North allowed the Soviet Union to withdraw its forces in 1948: it was a different story in the South. Peasant-based guerilla warfare started in 1946 as the popular land reform committees set up after the defeat of Japan were brutally repressed. Between 1946 and the outbreak of war in June 1950, an estimated 100,000 people in South Korea were killed in what was to all intents and purposes a war of national liberation. The US could not withdraw since without its military and economic support, the Rhee regime would collapse overnight, with an incalculable political impact on Japan and the rest of South East Asia – a view shared by the Labour left:

> 'If she [the USA] allowed South Korea to be occupied without coming to her help then the prestige of the West in Asia would have suffered severely. The repercussions would have been felt in Malaya, Indo-China, Burma and indeed throughout South East Asia.'[35]

---

35. *Tribune*, 7 July 1950.

The issue then, in June 1950, was not who started the war, but the substance of it: and that was the ending of imperialist partition. As the North Koreans swept south, forcing the numerically superior and far better-armed American and South Korean troops to flee for their lives, the popular committees took over the state administration, purging it of the former collaborationists and instituting widespread land reform. As South Korean forces fell back to a small enclave in the South, they butchered tens of thousands more in widely-reported atrocities. To this were added even more when, backed by huge US firepower, they moved back and over the 38th Parallel toward the border with China.

As it was to do in 1990 over the Iraqi occupation of Kuwait, the USA turned to the UN to provide a smokescreen for its intervention. The Labour Government supported it completely, committing 12,000 troops, the largest foreign contingent after the USA. In this action, the Government was enthusiastically supported by the Labour left; as a *Tribune* editorial put it on 30 June 1950 just after the start of hostilities:

> 'In the face of such action [the alleged North Korean invasion], the US government has in our view taken the correct and inevitable course. First, it has taken every step with the approval of the necessary majority in the UN Security Council. Second, it has made it clear that even if it fails to preserve the South Korean government, it will resist to the utmost Communist expansion anywhere else in the east.'

and added that the USA had:

> 'demonstrated that there is no possibility of Communist aggression succeeding by reason of Western appeasement. The West has shown that it has preferred to fight, if need be, and that is a lesson that will not be lost on the Russians.'

The following week, in an editorial entitled 'Some thoughts about Appeasement', *Tribune* opined:

> 'Of course the prospect of war by atom bomb or hydrogen bomb opens up a vista of infinite horrors. But they are not the only

horrors. For example in the last war, how many more people, Jews and others, were killed by the Nazis in their extermination camps than were directly killed by the use of atom bomb. The answer is 100 times more. It is worth pondering these figures in considering whether there is any short cut to peace, or whether appeasement pays.'[36]

This was of course little more than an incitement to use the bomb, presumably to help the 'prestige' of the West in Asia. In view of the evident character of the Rhee regime and the real nature of the war, bravely reported by journalists like Rene Cutforth, James Cameron, Alan Winnington and Wilfred Burchett, the revolting corruption of the Labour left seems almost staggering. Indeed, even more so when the use of nuclear weapons was actively considered on numerous occasions by the USA.

Labour re-introduced national service – again with the support of *Tribune* – initially for a period of 18 months, later extending it to two years. Rene Cutforth and James Cameron were subjected to abuse and vilification for reporting the absolute barbarity of the Rhee regime and the collusion of the Americans. The Cabinet discussed the possibility of prosecuting Alan Winnington, a Communist, for treason after he wrote a pamphlet *I saw the truth* about these brutalities; they were only dissuaded because the mandatory sentence for the offence is death.

In November 1950, as American forces aimed for the Chinese border with the clear indication that they would cross it if necessary, the People's Republic of China intervened. The combined Korean and Chinese forces drove the US and South Korean forces back down to the 38th Parallel, where a bloody stalemate ensued. The retreating Rhee regime carried out more reprisals, including a mass execution witnessed by British troops. The British ambassador made representations to the USA to 'dissuade the Korean authorities from running unnecessary risks' – the risk being 'an incident' if British troops were again subjected

---

36. *ibid.*

to the spectacle of mass executions.'[37] A Foreign Office official wrote back saying 'The continuing reports of "atrocities" and "political shootings" are, as you know, giving us a lot of trouble.'[38] The response was a much tighter military and political censorship. Hence it was not reported until later that Labour had indicated it would be prepared to consider supporting direct military action against China on two occasions – in May and September 1951. And if it boasted it had opposed the USA's use of nuclear weapons when Truman suggested it publicly at the end of November 1950, this meant little because it had no control. The USA never ruled out the use of nuclear weapons; in April 1951, bombs were despatched to Okinawa and Truman approved a request that they be available if there were further significant Chinese reinforcements. In September 1951, lone B-29 bombers made dummy runs over North Korea simulating a nuclear attack – that is, following the attack lines they had taken over Hiroshima and Nagasaki. The nature of these runs would have been obvious to North Korean radar operators – whether or not they were simulation, they could only guess.

When the war finally ground to a halt in 1953, some three million Koreans had been killed. But already by 1951, the US airforce had been grounded because there were no more targets for it to attack – everything North of the 38th Parallel had been utterly destroyed. Labour had even in this its last days shown an unquestioning determination to defend the world-wide interests of imperialism; the left's virulent support had destroyed any opposition. Only the CPGB took a remotely principled line and many of its meetings were violently broken up; but years of adaptation to the Labour Party had reduced its practical impact. On the other hand the non-Communist left echoed *Tribune*; the founders of the Socialist Workers Party (SWP), for

---

37. Quoted in J Halliday and B Cummings, *Korea – The Unknown War*, Viking, 1988, p137. This excellent book is also the source of the material below on dummy nuclear runs.
38. *ibid.*

instance, keen to protect the Labour Party and their alliance with its left wing, declared their opposition to North Korea, describing it as a Russian stooge. Political expediency came before the interests of the Korean people.

3.14 *Summary*

It is safe to say that without the Labour Government, the reconstruction of the world imperialist order would have been a far more hazardous proposition. For two crucial years, 1945-47, it provided the political and military lead in confronting liberation movements throughout the world. At that point, it handed the baton over to US imperialism, and concentrated on building up the British economy at the expense of the Empire. A Tory Government could not have achieved this: Churchill's leadership would have provided too naked an expression of British imperialist interests.

By basing British recovery firmly and squarely on the exploitation of the Empire, Labour's record turned into a consummation of the theory of 'socialist colonialism' discussed at Stuttgart in 1907, and enthusiastically approved by Ramsay MacDonald. Labour felt no compunction at exploiting the Empire in this way; racism was endemic within its leadership. When Hugh Dalton was offered the chance of becoming Colonial Secretary after the 1950 Election, he turned it down, noting in his diary: 'I had a horrid vision of pullulating, poverty-stricken, diseased nigger communities, for whom one can do nothing in the short run, and who, the more one tries to help them, are querulous and ungrateful.'[39]

Labour's foreign and colonial policy during these six years can now be seen as of far greater historical significance than anything it achieved domestically. Full employment has long since gone; nationalisation will also soon be a thing of the past, not to mention the welfare state. Yet on the foreign stage, Labour constructed the imperialist alliances which were eventually to destroy the Soviet Union; it kept Greece, Indonesia,

---

39. Quoted in Gupta, *op cit*, p336.

India, Pakistan and Malaya in the imperialist camp; it was responsible for wars in Viet Nam which were to claim the lives of millions. Labour never had to kill one British worker at home to rebuild British imperialism. But it had to kill untold thousands in the rest of the world, often with the enthusiastic support of its left wing. Hence those who seek to show that Labour played a progressive role between 1949 and 1951 can only do so on the racist assumption that the lives of the colonial people are of far less importance than those of British workers.

Labour Prime Minister, James Callaghan, meeting architect of apartheid Prime Minister Vorster – 1975

PART FOUR

Labour and British imperialism since 1951

4.1 Labour in opposition: 1951-64

The defeat of the Labour Government in 1951 was a prelude to the long imperialist boom of the 1950s and 1960s. The Conservative Government, free from the most pressing and immediate effects of the post-war crisis, set about establishing a neo-colonial solution to the problem of empire. This involved building up the bourgeois component in the national liberation movements, whilst suppressing ruthlessly any influence from the working class or peasantry; it was a process completely supported by Labour, as in Guyana and Kenya.

The first elections ever in British Guyana, under a Labour-inspired constitution, were held in April 1953, and resulted in a landslide victory for the mildly-reforming, non-racial Peoples' Progressive Party (PPP) under the leadership of Cheddi Jagan. The PPP extended trade union rights, reformed education, ended corrupt expenditure of money on colonial officials, and introduced basic social legislation. On 4 October, the Tories suspended the constitution, and sent in troops, alleging that the PPP were organising a communist takeover. At issue were the bauxite resources of the colony. The British TUC weighed in with its support, accusing the PPP of waging a communist policy, of supporting the World Federation of Trade Unions as opposed to the CIA International Congress of Free Trade Unions, and of endeavouring to destroy the ManPower Citizens Association, a company union. The Labour

Party NEC then banned affiliates from inviting PPP speakers to present their case, so effectively isolating them.

The Kenyan people had already served notice during the life-time of the Labour Government that they wanted their freedom. In 1952, following the suppression of the East African TUC, the KAU was also banned, and trade unionists and political leaders were gaoled. With the normal channels of bourgeois protest exhausted, the struggle of the Kenyan Land and Freedom Army – the Mau Mau – started. From the outset, Labour's support for British imperialism was assured: James Griffiths declared:

'from the beginning we have given the Government our fullest support in any steps that are required to suppress Mau Mau.'[1]

Labour might distance itself from what it regarded as Tory 'excesses' but only because such 'excesses' 'will have the effect of creating in Kenya a whole people who will be resentfully against us in the future.'; Griffiths himself was concerned at 'the danger of driving all the Kikuyu people into the hands of the Mau Mau', and thought it of 'the utmost importance' that there be 'a responsible political organisation to which the Africans can look for leadership' – that is, a bourgeois leadership willing to accept a neo-colonial settlement. Fenner Brockway, for the left, concurred; he found the Mau Mau 'an ugly and brutal form of extreme nationalism', and urged the Government to 'accept the offers of African leaders to take their part' in the campaign against the Mau Mau. The suppression of the Mau Mau allowed British imperialism and Jomo Kenyatta to find this neo-colonial solution; one which still leaves the Kenyan people dependant on imperialism today.

Labour played the same refrain during Suez, cautioning the Tories against playing into 'communist' and 'extremist' hands. Nasser's coup in 1952 had given the Tories no option but to move troops out of Suez – no longer was there a puppet government which might protest but do nothing. When in 1956 Nasser nationalised the Suez Canal to

---

1. Quoted in E Abrahams, *Fight Racism! Fight Imperialism!* No 32, *op cit.*

help pay for the Aswan Dam project, Gaitskell denounced the action as 'high-handed and totally unjustifiable', comparing Nasser to Hitler and Mussolini, and urging the supply of more arms to the Zionists. However, as the crisis developed, and it became apparent that there was not to be any US support for military action, Labour ruled it out, and moved to criticise the Tories' tactics, arguing that if the Government used force, 'they will leave behind in the Middle East such a legacy of distrust and bitterness towards the West that the whole area will be thrust almost forcibly under Communist control. This is the greatest danger of all.'[2]

Hence, when the invasion came in October 1956, Labour condemned it, not because of the violation of Egyptian sovereignty, or because of the slaughter of Egyptian civilians, but because the Government had lost an opportunity to attack the Soviet Union when the latter moved troops into Hungary.

4.2   Back in Office 1964-70

By 1964, when Labour returned to office with a slender majority, Britain's dominant position in relation to its European competitors had disappeared. Rates of industrial growth, investment and increases in productivity lagged as capital was preferentially exported to where a quicker profit could be found. Labour's answer was the rejuvenation of the economy through the 'white heat' of a 'technological revolution'; however it continued to act as a very junior partner of the USA in defending world imperialist interests.

In Aden, Labour policy followed a now very familiar pattern: repression of the progressive wing of the national freedom struggle, cultivation of the reactionary side.[3] The National Liberation Front had been formed in 1962 to fight British-backed counter-revolution against the revolutionary republic established in North Yemen. The NLF

---

2. Quoted in *Fight Racism! Fight Imperialism!* No 64, November 1986.
3. Material and quotations drawn from B Hughes, 'The Labour Party and South Yemen', *Fight Racism! Fight Imperialism!* No 43, October 1984.

represented the peasantry and Adeni working class, and launched armed struggle in 1963. However, Labour was quite clear it needed to retain Aden as a military base when it came into office, and one of its first acts was, in Harold Wilson's words: 'preparing for inevitable martial take-over, suspension of the constitution and a declaration of a state of emergency.' Sir Richard Turnbull, who had supervised the defeat of Mau Mau was appointed High Commissioner. The NLF was outlawed, and soon after, so was trial by jury. Widespread torture was practised; when it was exposed by Amnesty International, George Brown as Foreign Secretary declared the policy 'had operated with considerable success, having provided information leading to the discovery of numerous arms caches and to the arrest of a large number of terrorists.'

Labour's attempts to cultivate relations with the feudal sultans and the Adeni bourgeoisie via the Front for the Liberation of South Yemen (FLOSY) were doomed as the expense of supporting 17,000 troops came to more than British imperialism could bear in the midst of serious balance of payment problems. On 30 November 1967, the British were finally driven from South Yemen.

Meanwhile, the Government was backing the US war against Viet Nam to the hilt[4], not least because at critical moments it was dependent on the USA to provide it with loans to fend off frequent attacks on sterling. There was direct support: the training of thousands of South Viet Namese in jungle warfare at a school in Malaya, paid for by the Foreign Office; supplying arms, radar, and hovercraft (for use in the Mekong Delta). Then there was the political support, complete and unconditional. The 1965 Party Conference voted to support the USA, a position put in the 1966 Election Manifesto. In June 1965, the USA commenced bombing Hanoi and Haiphong, with Wilson's sympathy and understanding expressed in a cablegram to President Johnson:

'I wholly understand the deep concern you must feel at the need to do anything possible to reduce the losses of young Americans in

---

4. Material and quotations drawn from S Palmer, *op cit.*

and over Viet Nam . . . our reservations about this operation will not affect our continuing support for your policy over Viet Nam.'

The sympathy also extended to that year's Labour Party Conference, as it obligingly voted down a resolution dissociating Labour from the USA. Two years later, Wilson was to express 'the sense of outrage' he felt at the news of the Tet offensive which so nearly came to victory. Even later on in 1974, Labour would continue to back the South Viet Namese puppet regime, eventually welcoming Nguyen Van Thieu, the puppet ruler, after his defeat in September 1975 and settling him in Wimbledon.

Throughout this, the Labour left acted spinelessly, concerned as they were with not being seen to split the Party, something of far greater concern to them and their careers than the slaughter in Viet Nam. The most honest statement from a Labour member was made by Bertrand Russell in a speech on 14 October 1965:

> 'When I compare the horrors of the Viet Nam war with the election manifesto of the Labour Government, I find myself confronted with the most shameful betrayal of modern times in this country. Hitler, at least, seldom professed humanity, but these men who now pollute the chairs of office professed, before election, the most noble and lofty ideals of human brotherhood . . . I can no longer remain a member of this so-called "Labour" Party, and I am resigning after 51 years.'

At the end of his speech, he tore up his membership card and called for a new party to be built.

Following Labour's defeat in 1951, the Tories had continued with the Central African Federation project; established in 1953, it collapsed ten years later because it could not control either what was to become Zambia or Malawi. It left the Southern Rhodesian settlers on their own, faced with a movement led by the newly-formed Zimbabwe African National Union (ZANU) and Zimbabwe African People's Union (ZAPU). A Labour mission was sent out in February 1965 to negotiate with the settlers, but made no progress. The only thing Labour made clear was that it would not use force to impose majority rule. This was a green light: Labour was using force in Aden at the time, and was backing the USA in Viet Nam. Wilson himself went to Salisbury (Harare) in October, only to be boycotted by the settlers; when he returned to Britain he told ZANU and ZAPU leaders to take a more realistic stand and not hope that Britain would defend the Africans' rights by force. The settlers took the message, and unilaterally declared independence on 11 November.

Wilson's response was to rule out any negotiations with the settlers, impose a series of sanctions, but also to repeat the assurance that no force would be used. Within months, he had backed down; 'talks about talks' started in early 1966; and, in December, he met white Prime Minister Ian Smith on HMS *Tiger*. The document presented for discussion was an abject capitulation to the racists; it made clear, contrary to previous practice, that independence need not be accompanied by universal franchise: 'The British Government has repeatedly said that majority rule could not come about immediately but should be reached through merit and achievement.'[5] It therefore proposed to establish a Royal Commission, which it conceded would have to sit 'for several years' to work out ways to end racial discrimination. Knowing that sanctions would be circumvented through Portuguese Mozambique or South Africa, the settlers felt safe in rejecting Labour's pusillanimous proposals. The sanctions that Wilson promised would work 'in weeks rather than months' never worked at all: it took the armed struggle of ZANU and ZAPU to force the settlers to Lancaster House in 1980.

With South Africa itself, Wilson was keen to retain trading relationships, arguing in very familiar terms that sanctions 'would harm the people we are most concerned about, the Africans and those whites fighting to maintain some standard of decency.'[6] One of the first actions of the 1964 Government was to continue the supply of

---

5. Quoted in P Foot, *op cit*, p266.
6. Quoted in C Brown, 'The Labour Party and South Africa', *Fight Racism! Fight Imperialism!* No 30, June 1983.

Buccaneer bombers despite a commitment to stop them; the subsequent arms ban did not prevent the supply of landrovers and other para-military equipment. By 1967, South Africa was Britain's second largest export market, and Crosland could write: 'Our concern to see this valu-able trade develop and to avoid any economic confrontation with South Africa has been repeatedly made clear in Parliament and the UN'[7], and indeed it was, as Britain vetoed any resolution calling for a mandatory trade embargo. This period saw a rapid growth in British investment in apartheid, as domestic profitability fell: from £30 million a year in 1964 such investment rose to £70 million in 1969. In 1968, Tony Benn signed a contract with Rio Tinto Zinc for the illegal extraction of 7,500 tons of uranium from the Rossing mine in Namibia, an episode which never seriously damaged his later image as a leader of the left.

With one exception, there was no significant organised opposition to the Government's support for apartheid, especially in comparison with the movement against its policy over Viet Nam. This was because the character of the Anti-Apartheid Movement (AAM) was quite different to that of the Viet Nam Solidarity Committee: the former was tied to the Labour Party, and anything it did was circumscribed by the need to protect the interests of Labour.[8] Hence, although several government ministers were members, the AAM refused to take action against them even though their own Government actively encouraged links with apartheid. The only effective action against British links was in fact organised outside of the AAM, and in face of its opposition: the Stop the Seventy Tour Campaign against a visit from the Springboks rugby and cricket teams. It organised large and militant demonstrations against the rugby team between November 1969 and January 1970, drawing tens of thousands of people into active campaigning against apartheid for the first time, and forced Labour to 'persuade' the MCC to cancel the cricket tour organised for the summer of that year. After the campaign ended, the AAM subsided into inactivity, and distinguished itself only by its

---

7. *ibid.*
8. Drawn from C Brickley, T O'Halloran and D Reed, *South Africa – Britain Out of Apartheid, Apartheid out of Britain*, Larkin, 1986, pp25-29.

sectarian hostility to the most radical sections of the Southern African liberation movements. Hence, to the bitter end, it refused to give any support to ZANU in Zimbabwe whatsoever, and only under extreme pressure would it acknowledge the existence of the Pan Africanist Congress of Azania or sections of the Black Consciousness Movement.

Its irrelevance continued into the next Labour administration. In 1975, Labour nationalised British Leyland; when workers in its South African plants sought support in a unionisation drive, the Government refused to support them, saying that the issue was left to the 'commercial judgement' of the local management. At the end of 1976, total British investment in South Africa stood at just short of £11 billion, 50 per cent of total foreign investment. In January the following year, through its representative on the IMF Board, it agreed a loan to the apartheid state. Just to put the record straight, the British Ambassador declared in a broadcast in March 1977 'In particular, I must remind you that the only four occasions on which my Government, Britain, has exercised the veto in the Security Council during the life of the present Government has been in favour of South Africa.'[9] What more could be said?

4.3   Labour and Ireland from 1969 [10]

But if there is one thing for which the 1964 Labour Government is remembered, it is the despatch of troops to the Six Counties of Ireland. The sectarian statelet had come under increasing challenge from the mid-1960s onward, as the Nationalist people organised to demand an end to gerrymandering and other forms of discrimination. The widely-televised spectacle of the RUC violently batoning a Civil Rights march on 5 October 1968 in Derry was one landmark in the developing mass movement, followed in March 1969 by the election to Parliament of Bernadette Devlin as a united anti-Unionist candidate. Throughout the early summer of 1969, there were repeated confrontations between the

---

9. Quoted in C Brown, *Fight Racism! Fight Imperialism!* No 30, *op cit*.
10. Material drawn from D Reed, *op cit*, pp113ff.

Nationalist people unwilling to accept the cosmetic reforms they had been offered, and a Unionist Government incapable of giving any more. When the Stormont Government refused to ban the Apprentice Boys' annual march round Derry on 12 August, the people of the Bogside served notice that they would defend their community. Barricades went up on the night before: for three days the RUC attempted to break through using armoured cars against a hail of petrol bombs (43,000 bottles went missing from the local dairy). On 14 August, exhausted, the RUC admitted defeat, and that afternoon British troops arrived to relieve them. The following day, the Army was deployed in the Falls Road, after a night of unbridled Loyalist terror supported by RUC armoured cars and B-Specials had failed to crush the resistance of the Nationalist people despite claiming six lives.

Labour had sent in the troops firstly to contain the insurrection in Derry, and only after that to Belfast to prevent the possible outbreak of civil war. Without the enormous resistance there would have been no talk of reforming the Northern Ireland statelet; time would tell that it could never amount to any more than talk. Once again, however, Labour had found sycophants to its left who were prepared to support its despatch of troops – the Tribune group, of course, the CPGB, Militant and the International Socialists (now the SWP). This would be a foretaste of the future, where the numerically significant forces on the left would show themselves at best indifferent to, and often in support of, British imperialist policy in the occupied Six Counties.

By the time Labour returned to government in 1974 after the 'Who Rules Britain?' election, a war of national liberation in Ireland was in full swing. The British Army had been as ineffective as the RUC in forcing the Republican minority to submit: the Tories had introduced internment on 9 August 1971, with the accompanying physical and psychological torture of the first detainees. A protest demonstration on 30 January 1972 in Derry turned into Bloody Sunday as 14 civilians were murdered by the Paratroop regiment. The resultant explosion forced Heath to suspend Stormont on 20 March and later replace it with the Sunningdale power-sharing agreement. This was unacceptable to the Loyalists, who threatened to destroy it; in May 1974, the threat became a reality as the Ulster Workers' Council organised a general strike to bring it down. With the Army unwilling to intervene, Labour caved in and abandoned power-sharing, leaving it no option but to strengthen direct rule. Within short order, it presided over the framing of Judith Ward, the Guildford 4, the Maguire 7 and the Birmingham 6, and passed the Prevention of Terrorism Act in the wake of the Birmingham bombings at the end of the year.

Not until December 1975, however, was internment finally ended, following an agreement between the Republican movement and the Government earlier in the year. It was replaced by judicial internment, carried on through the juryless Diplock Courts. Labour's strategy was one of complete repression: the widespread use of torture to extract 'confessions' from detainees; the use of Diplock courts to almost guarantee a conviction, and the ending of Special Category status, so as to criminalise the prisoners. The aim was to establish sufficient political stability to allow the return of government to the Six Counties – 'Ulsterisation'.

Torture was officially sanctioned by the McGonigal judgement, which ruled that 'a certain roughness of treatment' of detainees was quite acceptable, and certainly different from 'torture'. Between 1975 and 1979, between 93 per cent and 96 per cent of all cases appearing before Diplock courts resulted in conviction; of these, between 70 per cent and 90 per cent depended either wholly or mainly on a 'confession'. After Roy Mason became Secretary of State for Northern Ireland at the end of 1976, the use of torture became even more extensive. By autumn 1977, allegations about its use were so widespread that an ITV programme was broadcast on the subject. Mason, who had earlier described the consequent injuries to prisoners as 'self-inflicted', dismissed it as 'cheque-book television', but the following week Amnesty International announced it would send a team to investigate. Its report, published in May 1978, concluded that there was widespread maltreatment of suspects, and recommended a public inquiry. This call was dismissed by Mason, who set up a private inquiry to ensure that there was as little publicity as possible over the affair. Torture of detainees continued.

Mason was also responsible for the use of SAS shoot-to-kill tactics which cost the lives of 11 people between late 1977 and 1978, including several unarmed civilians. But it was the criminalisation policy which was to galvanise nationalist opposition once again. On 14 September 1976 Kieran Nugent became the first political prisoner to refuse to wear the prison clothing that became obligatory with the ending of Special Category Status. By March 1978, over 300 prisoners were on protest, all subjected to constant beating from the prison warders in an effort to make them submit. By this time, they had also been forced to start the 'no wash' protest because leaving their cells for a shower or to use the toilet had become without fail an occasion for a vicious beating. Outside, working class women had started to organise support for the prisoners 'on the blanket', forming themselves into local Relatives' Action Committees. By 1978, regular demonstrations of over 10,000 people were being held – the attempt to isolate the Republican movement had ended in failure.

Not that Labour was daunted. In an attempt to keep themselves in office over the winter of 1978, they offered a deal to the Loyalist MPs, offering them extra parliamentary seats in return for their support against the Tories. This vulgar horse-trading was to continue in March 1979, when they vainly sought the support of both Gerry Fitt of the SDLP and the Irish independent MP Frank Maguire to defeat a motion of no confidence. They had become the victims of the policy they had embraced so enthusiastically in the years beforehand.

4.4 Labour imperialism during the Thatcher years

Forced into the election of June 1979, Labour lost support from significant sections of the poorer working class – black people, low-paid public sector workers, and, of course, Irish people. A campaign of disruption of rallies addressed by Labour leaders exposing the record of torture and criminalisation, and led by the Revolutionary Communist Group (RCG), obtained significant publicity; in contrast, the rest of the left called for a vote for Labour, once again showing their contempt for the struggles of the oppressed. The advent of the Tories signalled that

British imperialism was in no mood for compromise, and neither were the prisoners. The first hunger-strike ended with an agreement which the British Government almost immediately betrayed, setting the scene for the second, started by Bobby Sands on 1 March 1981.

By the time it was over, ten men had been murdered. Michael Foot, now leader of the Labour Party, had made clear that he stood full-square with the Government, to the extent of sending Don Concannon, shadow spokesman on Northern Ireland, to tell Bobby Sands on his deathbed that Labour did not support the demands of the hunger-strikers. This was at a time when Labour was supposed to be falling under the control of the left: not one Labour MP openly supported the five demands of the hunger strikers, and the only parliamentary protest came from an obscure right-winger, Patrick Duffy.

Whenever Ireland has become an issue since, Labour has proved it to be above party interest. In 1982, Michael Foot supported the banning of Gerry Adams and Danny Morrison after they were invited to London by Ken Livingstone. In 1983, Kevin McNamara, Labour spokesperson on Northern Ireland, opposing the renewal of the Prevention of Terrorism Act (PTA), said: 'Ordinary decent coppers using ordinary decent police methods apprehended those responsible for the Birmingham outrage'[11], perhaps an unintentional confirmation that torture, forgery and perjury are 'ordinary decent police methods'. At the end of 1987, Kinnock cautioned Charles Haughey against using the extradition issue to obtain reform of the Diplock courts. In 1988, Labour congratulated the Tories on the murder of the Gibraltar 3. It abstained on the vote to renew the PTA just after the European Court of Human Rights had ruled that the seven-day detention rule breached the Convention of Human Rights. In December, the NEC stated: 'the Party has never declared the Birmingham 6 or the Guildford 4 to be innocent. It does not believe the Party is in a position to declare them innocent' – not surprisingly, since they were convicted under a Labour Government.[12]

---

11. Quoted *ibid*, p408.
12. Decision of December 1988 NEC, quoted by Maxine Williams, *Fight Racism! Fight Imperialism!* No 84, February 1989, p5.

The stance that Labour adopted during both the Falklands and Gulf Wars then is no surprise, no accident, no expression of a rightward drift amongst its leadership. Michael Foot said of the Task Force in 1982: 'our first concern in the Labour Party as in the country as a whole must be for their safety and success' [13]; without his benediction, it is unlikely that the force could have been sent. The Labour left wanted neither to condemn British imperialist ambitions nor undermine their left wing credentials; hence Tony Benn argued for more time for economic sanctions to work, but made clear he agreed on fundamentals: 'There is unanimity in the House on the question of opposing the aggression of the Junta. There is also unanimity on the right of self-defence against aggression.' [14]

This refrain was to be familiar during the lead-up to the Gulf War. The Labour leadership was if anything more rabid than Thatcher: Kaufman as Shadow Foreign Secretary denounced the Tories as 'slack, lax and negligent' in their response to the invasion of Kuwait (this was at a time when Thatcher was warning Bush not 'to go wobbly'), and boasted that Labour had insisted on Iraqi war reparations fully one month before the Tories took it up. Benn meanwhile wanted more time for economic sanctions – which are still in place, and which are now killing thousands of Iraqi children – whilst making clear that he opposed Iraqi 'aggression' against British interests. During both wars, Benn and his allies played that familiar role of the Labour left: accepting the substance of the leadership's position – protection of British imperial interests – whilst choosing to distance themselves from the means with some pacific and even democratic phrases. Their role allows others outside the Labour Party to then praise them, magnify their significance, pretend that they represent the true working class heart of the Party, and thus justify their own continuing alliance with it. Thus it was that during both wars, no significant section of the left were prepared to act independently of Benn, because their need for an alliance with Labour forced them to protect it against the emergence of any separate movement.

---

13. Quoted in Editorial, *Fight Racism! Fight Imperialism!*, No 20, June 1982.
14. Quoted *ibid*.

4.5 *The Labour Party and British imperialism: a summary*

Orwell may have had many political deficiencies, but he knew hypocrisy and political corruption when he saw them. He was always quite frank about the nature of the Labour Party; in *The Lion and the Unicorn*, he argued that Labour 'has never possessed a genuinely independent policy', and that 'This meant that all through the critical years it was directly interested in the prosperity of British capitalism. In particular it was interested in the maintenance of the British Empire, for the wealth of England was drawn largely from Asia and Africa. The standards of living of the trade union workers, whom the Labour Party represented, depended indirectly on the sweating of Indian coolies.'[15] Hence his earlier description of the humbug of left wing politics, which could casually describe Britain as a democracy, and ignore the slavish conditions of those whose exploitation provided the basis for that democracy – the colonial oppressed. Orwell saw the connection between imperialism and political corruption within the 'democratic' or 'socialist' movement. That this is a rare insight can be gathered from its exclusion from the vast majority of histories of the Labour Party.

Labour, in or out of office, whatever the decade, wherever the colony or dependency, took as its starting point the defence of Britain's imperial interests. Labour has never adopted an anti-imperialist position on any issue. More than that: it has never ever had a significant anti-imperialist current within it. From time to time, the left wing may have protested against the methods; it has never disputed the aims. It has never championed the struggle of the Irish people. It never stood up for the masses of India. It regarded French Senegalese troops in the Ruhr as 'black savages', had contempt for 'Chinks' in 1927, mused on the use of the atom bomb in Korea in 1950, vilified the Mau Mau a few years later. In other words, its political culture was as corrupt as the leadership's, although the language it used might sometimes have been more democratic and pacific.

Labour then has been first and foremost an imperialist party, with an

---

15. G Orwell, *The Lion and the Unicorn*, Penguin, 1982, p96.

imperialist and racist culture. That culture is the culture of privilege, of a section of the working class whose conditions of life are maintained through the parasitic relationship of British imperialism to the rest of the world. It is corrupt and corrupting; it extends beyond the Labour Party to affect those who then seek to protect it, who themselves reveal an 'utter boorish self-centred indifference to every living human struggle, that is the heart and soul of the imperialist psychology in the labour aristocracy and the petty bourgeoisie.' That privilege has been preserved against the interests of the oppressed through out the world; it has also been preserved against the interests of the mass of the British working class, as we shall now see.

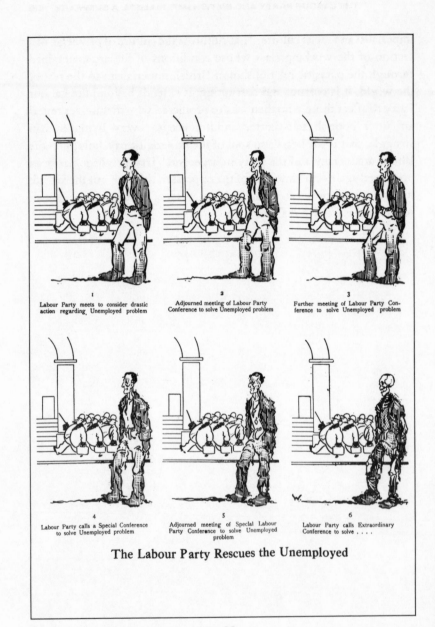

1. Labour Party meets to consider drastic action regarding Unemployed problem

2. Adjourned meeting of Labour Party Conference to solve Unemployed problem

3. Further meeting of Labour Party Conference to solve Unemployed problem

4. Labour Party calls a Special Conference to solve Unemployed problem

5. Adjourned meeting of Special Labour Party Conference to solve Unemployed problem

6. Labour Party calls Extraordinary Conference to solve . . . .

The Labour Party Rescues the Unemployed

Cartoon from *The Communist* 1921-22

PART FIVE

Labour and the working class 1918-45

5.1 *British imperialism between the Wars*

The period between the wars was one of painful and, in the end, only partial reconstruction of British manufacturing and industry. The effect on large sections of the working class was, however, enormous; by 1939, its structure had changed significantly. In addition, it created a huge reserve army of labour, an oppressed section of the working class ignored and isolated by the Labour Party and the TUC and organised only by Communists. During the late 1930s, as the economy boomed in the South East and the Midlands, the structure of the working class in these areas started to take on the features that are developed to such a high degree today, and which are a product of the most parasitic side of British imperialism.

On the face of it, the British economy had suffered lightly during the First Imperialist War compared to its main competitors such as France and Germany, which had experienced enormous destruction. It was still a creditor nation – its debt of $4.7 billion to the USA was more than balanced by credits of $8.6 billion if the Russian debts cancelled by the Bolsheviks are ignored. In addition, it had emerged as the supreme power in the Middle East, with a mandate over Palestine and with oil-rich Iraq firmly in its orbit.

But the underlying problems had not been resolved, and as European reconstruction started, so the uncompetitive nature of much of British industry became more and more apparent; its most significant feature, a major deterioration in export performance (see Table 8), brought considerable pressure on the balance of payments. No longer could these deficits be made up through overseas income, since a substantial proportion of overseas assets had been liquidated to help pay for the war effort. Although strenuous efforts were made to rebuild them, this required much borrowing on the open market: hence the phenomenon of 'lending long and borrowing short' – building up long-term assets through short-term borrowing. The nature of these assets was such that they could not be easily liquidated in the event of sudden financial shocks, so, with low levels of gold reserves, the financial structure of British imperialism was to be extremely shaky, as the events of 1931 were to prove.

Table 8 **The British Economy 1913-37** (£000,000) [1]

Year	National income at current prices	National income at 1913 prices	Exports & re-exports at 1913 prices	Imports at 1913 prices
1913	2265	2021	634.8	768.7
1921	4460	1804	368.3	493.4
1923	3844	1917	459.8	560.3
1925	3980	2070	540.7	770.0
1927	4145	2259	507.3	742.8
1929	4178	2319	521.1	758.2
1931	3666	2270	315.6	598.1
1933	3728	2422	304.3	492.7
1935	4109	2616	348.2	588.7
1937	4616	2728	395.0	680.6

1. Calculated from ed B Mitchell and P Deane, *op cit*, Cambridge, 1962, pp828-9 and 872-3; and from J Kuczynski, *op cit*, p131.

Following the brief inflationary boom of 1920, output did not substantially exceed the 1913 level until in the year following the defeat of the General Strike, 1927. However, whilst the level of imports matched that of 1913, that of exports and re-exports were down 20 per cent, a deficit which had to be compensated by what was in real terms a smaller surplus on invisibles. Put another way: whilst exports covered more than 80 per cent of the value of imports in 1913, in the 1920s this had fallen to about 70 per cent. The parasitic features of the British imperialist economy thus became more and more dominant.

Although there was a steady increase in productivity, this was achieved more through speed-up and the intensification of labour, or through concentration and cartelisation than it was through new investment, which in real terms stagnated. The series of 'more loom' disputes in the textile industry were an example: productivity was intensified through the simple device of making workers operate more looms. This led to a series of disputes which accounted for two-thirds of all days lost in strikes between 1926 and 1934. Industrial stagnation was then the norm for the 1920s: as the then Chancellor of the Exchequer, Churchill, stated in his budget speech on the eve of the General Strike:

'The basic industries of the country, those which employ the largest number of workpeople, nearly all continue obstinately depressed under their heavy burdens.[2]

It was those basic sectors on which the industrial wealth of British imperialism depended that suffered most: coal, iron and steel, textiles and shipbuilding; Palme Dutt cites evidence that overall, British industrial output averaged 80-88 per cent of its 1913 level between 1921 and 1926; national income as presented in Table 8 also includes the parasitic, luxury sectors which were already expanding. Hobsbawm also describes such stagnation:

'Between 1912 and 1938 the quantity of cotton cloth made in Britain fell from 8,000 million to barely 3,000 million square

---

2. Quoted in Palme Dutt, *Socialism and the Living Wage*, CPGB, 1927, p52.

yards; the amount exported from 7,000 million to less than 1,500 million yards. Never since 1851 had Lancashire exported so little. Between 1854 and 1913 the output of British coal had grown from 65 to 287 million tons. By 1938 it was down to 227 million and still falling. In 1913 12 million tons of British shipping had sailed the seas, in 1938 there was rather less than 11 million. British shipyards in 1870 built 343,000 tons of vessels for British owners, and in 1913, almost a million tons: in 1938 they built little more than half a million.'[3]

The effect on employment was dramatic: the labour force in the cotton industry fell by over half between 1912 and 1938 (from 621,000 to 288,000)[4], the number of miners from 1,200,000 in 1923 to 700,000 in 1938; more generally:

'At all times between 1921 and 1938 at least one out of every ten citizens of working age was out of a job. In seven out of those eighteen years at least three out of every twenty were unemployed, in the worst years one out of five. In absolute figures unemployment ranged from a minimum of rather over a million to a maximum (1932) of just under three million; at all events, according to official figures, which for various reasons understated it. In particular industries and regions the record was even blacker. At its peak (1931-2) 34.5 per cent of coalminers, 36.3 per cent of pottery workers, 43.2 per cent of cotton operatives, 43.8 per cent of pig-iron workers, 47.9 per cent of steelworkers, and 62 per cent – or almost two in three – of shipbuilders and ship-repairers were out of work.'[5]

Branson and Heinemann make the essential point, that Britain's privileged, imperialist position 'was also a source of weakness. The tendency of British investors to export capital to the colonies, rather than invest it in modernising production at home, had contributed to

3. E Hobsbawm, *Industry and Empire*, Pelican, 1969, p207.
4. *ibid*, p209.
5. *ibid*, pp208-09

the technical backwardness of the older basic industries in Britain, which by their very age included a great deal of obsolete plant . . . It was these industries which were hit hardest by the slump.'[6]

The overall impact of the slump on British imperialism was however less than in the USA or Europe, partly because it could turn to the protected markets of the Empire, partly because there was still the cushion of imperial tribute from overseas investment, even if at a lower level, and partly because basic industries had been anyway generally depressed beforehand. In specific areas, it was of course quite devastating: in the coalfields of Scotland and South Wales, the steel and coal regions on Northumberland and Durham, the cotton areas of Lancashire, not to mention any shipbuilding area, unemployment in the 1930s would be 30, 40 per cent and more; the peak in Jarrow when Palmer's shipyard closed was 80 per cent. 20 to 25 per cent of the population lived in areas which remained severely depressed until the war.

Recovery when it came was therefore patchy and localised, and presented new parasitic features. Firstly, growth was concentrated overwhelmingly in London, the Home Counties and the Midlands. Between 1932 and 1937, the number of insured workers in Greater London rose 14 per cent; in the same years, of the net increase of 644 factories, 532 were in the Greater London area.[7] These new factories were mainly in the luxury goods sector: vehicle manufacture, electrical trades, household goods. But the biggest increases in employment were in the distributive trades (up 807,000 from 1923 to 1937), public and private "services" (up 560,000), building and construction of public works (up 485,000). As against this, there was an overall increase in manufacturing employment of only 219,000.[8] 'Napoleon is said to have called Great Britain "a nation of shopkeepers"; by 1938 it seemed to be turning into a nation of shop assistants, clerks, waiters and machine attendants.'[9]

---

6. N Branson and M Heinemann, *Britain in the 1930s*, Panther, 1971, p13.
7. *ibid*, p81
8. Cole and Postgate, *op cit*, p605.
9. *ibid*, p609

The most visible sign of the boom of the 1930s was the growth of the middle class, for whose spending power much of the new industry catered. As in the 1980s, the extension of credit was to play a vital role in creating a new affluence for the middle class and small sections of the working class. This was particularly important for stimulating a housing boom which created the suburbia of Greater London, the Home Counties and the Midlands. This building formed a huge portion of Gross Domestic Capital Formation (GDCF): in 1913, 11.9 per cent of GDCF was made up of dwellings; in the 1930s, it was never less than 34.9 per cent, in 1932; and from 1934 to 1936 it exceeded 40 per cent, whilst in 1933 it was over 50 per cent. Net of dwellings, it was not until 1937 that GDCF was to exceed the 1913 level as a proportion of National Income. From 1931 to 1939, private industry built just short of two million new houses, whilst local authorities built less than 600,000.[10] The peak was in 1935, when private enterprise built over 287,000, seven times the number built by local authorities.

Most of these houses were built for sale: the period saw the transformation of the building society into the 'foremost investment agency in Great Britain.'[11] In 1913, Building Societies lent £9 million; in 1935, £135 million. Mortgage loans doubled between 1929 and 1936 (from £268 million to £587 million)[12], whilst the incurred debts were being paid off at £80 million per year. Cole and Postgate point to this as:

> ' . . . an immensely significant social phenomenon. In 1938, the "blackcoats" and the top layer of the manual working class, as well as the middle classes, largely bought their houses, instead of renting them.'[13]

The new municipal housing estates, too, benefitted the more privileged sections of the working class: their quality made them more expensive than private rented accommodation; they were also mainly located in

---

10. Branson and Heinemann, *op cit*, p222.
11. Cole and Postgate, *op cit*, p615.
12. Aldcroft and Richardson, *op cit*, p244.
13. *op cit*, p615.

city outskirts, so with the additional cost of travel to work, they were beyond the reach of the mass of the working class. In the meantime, 20,000 people in Liverpool and 200,000 in Glasgow lived three to a room[14], and there were still 5.7 million houses classed as slums.

The general effect of the crisis on real wages was far more serious for the worse-off sections of the working class, for a variety of reasons. First, there was a far greater pressure to cut money wages in the most backward industries such as coal mining and cotton manufactures. Second, such industries also had far more short-time working. Thirdly, the means test meant that many workers still employed in areas of high unemployment had to support relatives who were out of work. Hence, although prices fell throughout the period, and especially during the early 1930s, it was only those in steady employment, in areas of low unemployment, such as London, the Midlands and the South East, which benefitted.[15] For vast sections of the working class, little had changed since before the war, whilst for some, for instance in the mining and cotton industries, conditions had become distinctly worse.

The slump of 1929-31 was in fact to greatly accentuate the parasitic features of British imperialism. From covering 70 per cent of the value of imports in the 1920s, exports covered about 60 per cent in the 1930s, whilst the balance of invisible exports (including income on overseas investment) rose from just over 50 per cent of visible export income to just over 60 per cent on average. Despite the fact that there were substantial defaults on overseas loans with some being written off altogether, accumulated overseas investment fell only slightly, from £3,738 million in 1929 to £3,692 million in 1938 – possibly a slight rise in real terms. Once again, British usury provided a cushion; monopoly control of Empire food and raw material prices enabled it to make maximum advantage of the general fall in world prices for such commodities. Well might Hobson's description of the Home Counties in 1900 apply in 1938:

---

14. Branson and Heinemann, *op cit*, p203.
15. See Branson and Heinemann, *op cit*, pp150-164 for a good discussion of this point.

'Could the incomes expended in the Home Counties and other large districts of Southern Britain be traced to their sources, it would be found they were in large measure wrung from the enforced toil of vast multitude of black, brown or yellow natives, by arts not differing essentially from those which supported in idleness and luxury Imperial Rome.'[16]

And equally, Palme Dutt denounced:

' . . . the system of parasitism which has grown up to the most extreme point as the characteristic expression of British imperialism more than any other – the system of increasing dependence on world tribute alongside of actual productive decay. Imports unpaid by exports; declining role of industry and production; increasing role of the rentier and financial profits; declining exports and rising imports; decline of the basic industries (coal, iron, steel, engineering, shipbuilding, textiles) and the rise of the luxury "industries" (hotels, restaurants, shops, stores, artificial silk, motor cars, personal service, commerce, finance); mass unemployment and multi millionaires; falling real wages and rising super-tax incomes – this has been every year more and more the picture of modern capitalist Britain, a picture of rotten capitalist decay . . . '[17]

5.2   Labour between the Wars

As we have seen, the Labour Party was originally the creation of the skilled unions. By the end of the war, however, the new general unions, organising mainly semi-skilled workers, had gained much greater influence. These were not the general unions of 1889, but ones whose traditions were based on those of the old skilled unions, with a substantial bureaucracy which had gained extensive experience in running the affairs of the imperialist state during the Great War. Their

---

16. Quoted in Lenin, *Imperialism, op cit*, p280.
17. R Palme Dutt, *Crisis – Tariffs – War*, CPGB, 1932, p7.

leaders, epitomised by Ernest Bevin, were the new 'labour lieutenants' of the capitalist class, and it was they who were to ensure that the incipient revolutionary challenge to British imperialism in 1919-21 was stifled and then destroyed.

For two brief years, the British working class was in turmoil: demobilising soldiers mutinied, then rioted when they found no jobs in the 'land fit for heroes'. Even the police struck, to bring fears to the ruling class that events were moving beyond their control. In May 1920, dockers boycotted *The Jolly George* with its shipment of arms to Poland to help it in its war against the Bolsheviks. By summer, it was evident that the Government, having already sent troops to Archangel in the north and Baku in the south of the Soviet Union, was contemplating a far more extensive military commitment in support of Polish aggression. After the appalling slaughter of the war, there was no question of the working class tolerating a call to defend imperialist interests again, especially against the Soviet Union. On 13 August, a special joint Labour Party and TUC conference called for a general strike if such intervention took place, people like JH Thomas and Ramsay MacDonald taking the lead, for fear of losing control altogether. The Government backed off.

The end of 1920 spelled the end of the brief, inflationary post war boom. By March 1921, unemployment had leapt to over 11 per cent, compared to 2.4 per cent on average the previous year and 5.8 per cent in December. The Government announced it would terminate the subsidies which had enabled the coal mines to keep in operation from 31 March. The mine owners immediately announced new rates of pay, which would cut wages in some areas by up to 50 per cent. The miners refused to accept, and invoked the Triple Alliance of railway and transport workers to come to their aid. After two days of confusion, on Black Friday, 15 April, the union leaders called off a strike they had sanctioned on the Wednesday, and 'brought an epoch in the labour

---

17. R Palme Dutt, *Crisis – Tariffs – War*, CPGB, 1932, p7.

movement's history to an end.'[18] What would in effect have been a general strike was avoided. A million miners were left to fight alone, before being crushed three months later. Within months, they had been followed by the engineers.

Black Friday put the labour aristocracy back in control. By the time of Red Friday – 31 August 1925, when the threat of a general strike forced the Government to commit itself to nine months' subsidies for miners' wages – and the General Strike itself the following year, the Labour and trade union leadership were in a far more assured position. The defeat of the General Strike was a precondition for the re-establishment of some of the fortunes of British imperialism. Preparing the confrontation with meticulous care, the British ruling class was confident that it could rely on the official labour movement to deliver the final blow. The General Council of the TUC, mindful of its obligations to British imperialism and its constitution, duly obliged: the miners were to fight on for another six months, under constant attack from the leadership of the Labour Party. The organised working class was to play no further significant role between the wars.

5.3   The struggle of the unemployed

This did not mean the end of all resistance to the effects of the reconstruction of British imperialism, but it did mean that it had to be organised from outside the official movement. In practice, it fell to the Communist-led National Unemployed Workers' Committee Movement (NUWM) to mount any challenge. As in 1889 or 1913, the official movement was to stand against the interests of the poorer sections of the working class and seek to isolate them. And equally, it was to take revolutionaries to give expression to their demands and to organise them into any kind of force.

---

18. At greater length, Cole argued that Black Friday brought the 'period of post war industrial militancy to a decisive end', and that the impact of the defeat was compounded by the onset of the slump which saw unemployment soar from 5% in 1920 to 17% in 1921. (GDH Cole, *A History of Socialist Thought, op cit*, vol 4, Part 1, p430).

There had already been a number of riots and demonstrations at the end of the war over unemployment; in October 1920, a demonstration in support of London mayors lobbying the Ministry of Health for better treatment of the unemployed was viciously attacked by the police. A special joint conference of the Labour Party and TUC was held in January 1921 to discuss unemployment:

> 'The conference was to report back on the feelings of Labour Party and trade union members about taking "direct action" on unemployment. Yet the meeting place was kept secret, and a motion passed against hearing from the unemployed themselves. Strike action was rejected, and people simply advised to join the Labour Party. Jimmy Thomas, the right-wing leader of the railwaymen, was in the chair and refused to allow any motion other than an officially prepared one to be put. The meeting ended in uproar caused by delegates incensed by Thomas's ruling, and was followed by a march by 10,000 workless from outside the congress hall (the venue had not been a very well-kept secret) to Hyde Park .'[19]

Right from the beginning, the official movement had made its position clear; not surprisingly, Wal Hannington described the conference as 'not only an absolute farce but an abdication.'[20] On 15 April 1921, Black Friday, delegates from local unemployed committees met to discuss the formation of a national movement. 'Even as the unemployed movement was being established, then, the trade union leaders were demonstrating that they had no real support to offer fellow trade unionists in, let alone out of, work.'[21]

One of the first acts of the new movement was to organise a march from London to Brighton in the summer where the Labour Party Conference was meeting; a deputation which addressed the conference bitterly attacked both Labour and trade union leadership, demanding some action: all they got was a collection from the delegates. Reflecting

---

19. R Croucher, *We Refuse to Starve in Silence*, Lawrence and Wishart, 1987, p39.
20. ibid, p40.
21. *ibid.*

on this, one of the founders of the NUWM, Albert Hawkins appealed to the official movement to accept the NUWM as an affiliate body, arguing that 'Either the movement will take a recognised place in the ranks of the organised workers, or it will develop in the future upon independent and antagonistic lines. Whichever happens will depend on the attitude of the Labour Party.'[22]

Yet Labour was already showing its attitude in Poplar. The Poplar Board of Guardians since the end of the war had paid outdoor relief at a rate adequate to support the unemployed – much higher than the accepted norm. The growth in unemployment in 1920-21 meant that either it cut these rates, or defaulted on payments to certain Metropolitan funds. The Guardians, led by George Lansbury, chose the latter course, and were imprisoned for their pains. Throughout, they had massive local working class support, which forced the Government to introduce a scheme whereby funds were diverted from affluent middle class boroughs to the poorer one. But this did not prevent the Labour leadership attacking their stand, and when Labour did less well than expected in the 1922 Election, JH Thomas argued:

'Of course many of our political opponents will construe the election as a rebellion on the part of the people against the Labour policy . . . I do not interpret the result as a determination on the part of the people not to trust Labour, but I do frankly admit that it is a revolt against the kind of Poplar method of administration, which certainly alarmed people.'[23]

Tones very familiar to us from the last ten years or so! In response, Lansbury argued that: 'Sooner or later the Labour Party must face all the implications of administrative responsibility. The workers must be given tangible proof that Labour administration means something different from Capitalist administration, and in a nutshell this means diverting wealth from wealthy ratepayers to the poor. Those who pretend that a sound Labour policy can be pursued either nationally or

---

22. A Hawkins, *Labour Monthly*, November 1922, p277.
23. Quoted in *Labour Monthly*, June 1922, p383.

locally without making the rich poorer should find another party.'[24]

But in the conflict between Lansbury's hopes and sordid reality, reality triumphed as always. Poplar was isolated, no other councillors being prepared to court illegality, and when in 1925 the High Court ruled that Poplar would have to cut the rates it paid to its council workers, Lansbury succumbed. Forgetting his own advice of three years before, Lansbury pleaded successfully for the Poplar workers not to strike, the start of an odyssey which was to lead him to urge Labour councils to apply the means test – but humanely!

In late 1922, the NUWM organised the first national hunger march: throughout the winter, marches from various localities arrived in London, to be greeted by large demonstrations. The constant pressure saw the TUC make a small concession by establishing a Joint Action Committee with the NUWM; the last thing it was intended to do, or in fact did, was organise action, joint or otherwise.

Although unemployment had fallen somewhat by the time of the first Labour Government of 1924, it was still in excess of 10 per cent. The Government instituted some reforms to unemployment insurance: the period of benefit was extended from 26 to 41 weeks, and the weekly rates were improved. On the other hand, a clause in the relevant Bill allowed benefit to be refused if it was felt that the claimant was not genuinely seeking work; the 'Not genuinely seeking work' clause was to be used shortly to exclude hundreds of thousands from receiving benefit. However, the Government did not change the situation whereby outdoor poor relief could be offered as a loan or in kind; nor did it abolish the Guardian's discretion in refusing outdoor relief and offering the workhouse.

It was the Blanesburgh Unemployment Insurance Committee, set up in November 1925, and which reported at the beginning of 1927, which was to herald a vicious attack on the unemployed. Benefits were to be reduced, savagely so for those in the 18-21 age range, and contributions were to be raised to help reduce the insurance fund debt.

---

24. *ibid*, p388.

More seriously, the system of extended benefit, whereby claimants under certain conditions could get more than 26 weeks' benefit in any one year, was to be abolished; instead, claimants might be entitled to a new 'transitional' benefit provided they had made more than 30 contributions in the previous two years. This would eliminate seasonal workers and the long-term unemployed, since the entitlement to 'transitional' benefit would be reviewed every 13 weeks to determine whether the 30 contributions rule still applied. Stringent conditions were attached to the receipt of normal benefit: in particular, the 'Not genuinely seeking work' clause was stiffened by requiring claimants to give positive evidence of seeking work. Finally, it disallowed benefit for strikers completely.

Workers whose benefit had terminated would under normal circumstances have recourse to Poor Law relief; the Committee proposed that those who were struck off benefit as a result of their proposals should be prevented from obtaining such Poor Law relief:

'We understand that the Poor Law Acts and regulations made thereunder prohibit, except in special cases, the unconditional outdoor relief of able-bodied persons, and although the Minister of Health has found it necessary, during the extreme post-war depression, to assent to a widespread use of the regulation permitting unconditional relief in special cases, we think ... that in so far as it deals with the able-bodied unemployed, poor law relief should retain the deterrent effect which now attaches to it, or may be applied thereto.'[25]

What made this so outrageous was that there were three Labour representatives on the Committee, all of whom signed the report: Frank Hodges, former secretary of the Miners' Federation, AE Holmes, and Margaret Bondfield, a member of the TUC General Council, and to become Minister of Labour in the 1929-31 Labour Government. A special joint conference of the Labour Party and the TUC in April 1927, called under pressure to discuss the report, ruled a motion of censure on

---

25. Quoted in W Hannington, *Unemployed Struggles*, EP Publishing, 1977, p171.

the three submitted by the Miners' Federation out of order, and in the end merely called on the Parliamentary Labour Party to try to amend it.

At the same time, the Conservative Government sought to bring the local Boards of Guardians which administered Poor Law relief under more centralised control. Agitation by the NUWM had forced many Boards to use their discretionary powers over the distribution of relief in favour of the unemployed. Elected representatives to the Boards were replaced by appointed commissioners, who were to practice a ruthless economy.

The effect of these changes were dramatic. Between March 1927 and March 1928, 441,000 people were disqualified from receiving unemployed benefit; another 205,000 were disqualified in the next four months, most on the grounds of 'not genuinely seeking work', by which time one and a half million people were thrown on to Poor Law relief.[26] Yet this was a matter of indifference to the Labour and trade union barons. The defeat of the General Strike had allowed them to move decisively in isolating the Communists, issuing a series of bans and proscriptions. In March 1927, just before the special conference on the Blanesburgh report, the TUC unilaterally wound up the Joint Action Committee with the NUWM, General Secretary Citrine saying it would not serve any useful purpose. When in November 1927 the NUWM organised the second national hunger march, made up of miners from South Wales – there were by this time 350,000 miners out of work – the TUC and Labour Party circulated affiliates instructing them not to support it.

In September 1927, the TUC opened discussions with some industrialists who represented the monopoly or cartelised sections of British industry, led by Sir Alfred Mond, founder of the new ICI. In a letter to the TUC he wrote: 'We realise that industrial reconstruction can only be undertaken with the co-operation of those empowered to speak for organised labour ... We believe that the common interests which bind us are more powerful than the apparent divergent interests that

---

26. *ibid*, p176.

separate.'[27] The General Council concurred with the Mond group that the tendency towards rationalisation and trustification in industry 'should be welcomed and encouraged'. Although no formal machinery arose from the discussions, the talks, whose direction were supported at the 1928 TUC, gave a clear indication of where the TUC's priorities lay. This self-same TUC in Swansea had to be protected from the unemployed by the police acting in co-operation with Henderson and Citrine.

The NUWM organised a further national hunger march, directed specifically against the 'Not genuinely seeking work' clause, starting in January 1929. Once again, the TUC and Labour leadership instructed local affiliates not to render any assistance. The Ministry of Health, responsible for administering Poor Law relief, weighed in by instructing local authorities to treat hunger marchers as 'casuals' or tramps; this meant that a series of regulations were to be applied:

i) every man had to be searched on entering the workhouse, and he had to give his name and address;

ii) the regulation diet could not be exceeded (two slices of bread and margarine and a cup of tea for supper and breakfast).

iii) no man could leave the institution on the day of entering.

iv) a task had to be performed next morning before leaving.

v) no smoking, singing or meetings could be held in the institutions.

Contingents set off from Scotland, Durham, Yorkshire, Liverpool, Manchester, South Wales and Plymouth; all refused to accept the Ministry of Health regulations, and faced every evening a battle over accommodation which they generally won. They encountered police sabotage, especially in Birmingham; but the final demonstration in London on 24 February mobilised tens of thousands of workers despite the opposition of the 'official' movement.

Six weeks later, the then Chancellor of the Exchequer, Winston Churchill, in his budget speech, extolled the virtues of Empire:

---

27. Quoted in A Bullock, *The Life and Times of Ernest Bevin*, vol 1, Macmillan, p393.

'The income which we derive each year from commissions and services rendered to foreign countries is over £65 million. In addition, we have a steady revenue from foreign investments of close on £300 million a year ... That is the explanation of the source from which we are able to defray social services at a level incomparably higher than that of any European country or any country.'[28]

Very little of it seemed to get to the unemployed.

5.4   The unemployed and the 1929-31 Labour Government

Within three weeks, the second Labour Government had come into office. Nothing of substance was to change. Between June and September 1928, 58,000 claimants were disqualified for 'not genuinely seeking work'; the corresponding figures for the same four months of 1929 under Labour were nearly 80,000. Arthur Greenwood as Minister for Health proved equally vicious as his Ministry of Labour counterparts. He opposed an established scale of Poor Law relief, leaving it entirely to the discretion of the Boards of Guardians. He insisted on the continuation of 'test and task' work by able-bodied claimants – a form of forced labour which was a condition for obtaining relief. Lastly, he threatened to remove Boards of Guardians which discontinued the collection of relief debts incurred by miners. This was particularly odious. Miners who had been locked out in the great struggles of 1921 and 1926, or lost their jobs as a consequence, had often received poor relief in the form of a loan. Their wages savagely reduced when they were able to get work, they were frequently incapable of repaying such debts. Some Labour-dominated Boards had stopped trying to deduct the repayments; when they applied to the Labour Government for the cancellation of the debt, they were threatened with surcharge and suspension.

In February 1930, the NUWM organised a further march against the

---

28.   Quoted in R Palme Dutt, *The Crisis of Britain, op cit*, p80.

'Not genuinely seeking work' clause in the light of the Government's refusal to abolish it. Greenwood followed the example of his Tory predecessor in ruling that the marchers were to be treated as 'casuals', with as little success. Although smaller than its predecessors, it was during the march that the Government finally abolished the 'Not genuinely seeking work' clause; the final demonstration on 1 May was estimated at some 50,000 strong.

Under Labour, unemployment soared as capitalist rationalisation was officially encouraged; by December 1930, it had reached 2.6 million, nearly 20 per cent of the workforce. The Government appointed the Gregory Commission to study the solvency of the unemployment insurance scheme; it reported in June 1931 with a whole series of proposals limiting benefits and eligibility to them, to bring annual savings of £42 million. On behalf of the Government, Margaret Bondfield said: 'The Government agree in principle with the recommendations of the Royal Commission and we propose to place before the House proposals to give legislative effect substantially to these recommendations.' This took the form of the Anomalies Act; passed into operation in October 1931, it resulted in the disallowance of benefit to 77,000 claimants within six weeks, and 134,000 by the end of the year.

However, it was the report of the May Committee that spelt the end of the Government: recommending a 20 per cent cut in unemployment benefit together with the application of a means test for the extension of that benefit, cuts in wages for teachers, civil servants and the armed forces and sundry other economies, it forced the Government to act to balance the budget. The final cabinet vote, on a 10 per cent cut in benefit, gave a small majority in favour; but the condition of US bank loans to bail out the Government was their unanimous support, and on that basis, MacDonald dissolved it.

5.5   The unemployed and the National Government

The provisional National Government took over on 8 September; the day before, Citrine had once more called in the police to protect the TUC Congress in Bristol as 20,000 workers protested outside. Huge demonstrations of the unemployed took place up and down the country, organised by the NUWM: 50,000 in Glasgow, fighting off police attacks, 30,000 in Manchester. The *Daily Herald*, whose editorial policy was now firmly controlled through Odham's Press by Citrine and Bevin, condemned them: 'The remedy is in [the unemployed's] hands. Not in rioting and futile demonstrations, not in pointless collisions with the police, who are also victims, but in a determined effort to win the election for Labour.'[29]

Throughout September and October, huge demonstrations of the unemployed continued, frequently attacked by the police. Naval ratings mutinied on 12 September in protest at a shilling a day cut in wages, which amounted to a 20 per cent cut; they were quickly deemed a 'special case', and the cut greatly reduced. Teachers and civil servants too demonstrated; their cuts were limited to 10 per cent. The Government also pressed ahead with a 10 per cent cut in unemployment benefit, reducing the allowance for an adult man from 17s to 15s 3d, that for his wife from 9s to 8s, although the children's allowance of 2s was left untouched. But the main economy was in the application of the means test. Unemployment benefit was now automatically cut off after 26 weeks, to be replaced by a new 'transitional benefit'; this transitional benefit would only be granted after an exhaustive test of the means of the family by the Poor Law authority, and could not exceed unemployment benefit.

On 8 October, the day after the benefit cuts took place, 150,000 marched in Glasgow, and three days later 100,000 in London. Firehoses and mounted police failed to disperse 80,000 in Manchester; there were baton charges in Port Glasgow on 15 October, and in London and Cardiff the next day. On 27 October, the General Election returned the National Government with a landslide, and on 12 November, the means test came into operation. More demonstrations, more police attacks: but it was the NUWM organising the protests, not the official movement. Between 12 November 1931 and 23 January 1932, 270,000 were excluded by the means test from claiming any benefit whatsoever;

---

29. Quoted in Cliff and Gluckstein, *op cit*, p161.

by 20 February, this had risen to 377,000. Some 900,000 of the unemployed were on transitional benefit, so that not more than half the unemployed were still drawing unemployment benefit.

The Public Assistance Committees (PACs) had extreme discretion in deciding the scale of transitional relief: in Lancashire, less than 16 per cent received the maximum, and a third were excluded altogether from the means test. It was this discretion that led to rioting in Birkenhead and Belfast in 1932. In Birkenhead, a demonstration protested the fact that the PAC rates were 3s below the maximum. It was viciously attacked by the police; four days of rioting and fighting with the police took place; the PAC raised its scales. Where PACs had been appointed from Labour-controlled authorities they tended to pay maximum transitional benefit and either ignore the means test or interpret it liberally. However, the Ministry of Health cracked down, and replaced some of the PACs with appointed commissioners to administer the test properly:

'One by one the other recalcitrant PACs drew in their horns and appeared to be toeing the line. West Ham made a public statement: "We were threatened with supersession, and in face of that threat we prefer to keep the poor under our own care and do what we can for them rather than hand them over to an arbitrary Commissioner from whom they could expect little humanity".'[30]

However, it must not be thought that Labour control of the local PAC necessarily meant greater sympathy for the plight of the unemployed, as the murder of Arthur Speight in Castleford, Yorkshire in the summer showed:

'During a demonstration to the PAC, the Labour representatives on the PAC voted against receiving a delegation from the unemployed and that evening the unemployed demonstrated to the Trades and Labour Council in protest at the attitude of the Labour representatives. When the Council broke up, shouting at the Labour

---

30. Branson and Heinemann, *op cit*, p38.

men became hostile, and the police (mainly from outlying districts) made a fierce baton charge which left women, men and children badly beaten and an NUWM member, Arthur Speight, dead.Several local leaders of the movement were arrested, and the following day the Labour magistrate refused to grant any adjournment to the severely injured defendants and proceeded to sentence them immediately.'[31]

A further national march was organised for September and October: it coincided with the huge battle in Birkenhead, which was followed by one in Belfast, where for the first and only time ever, Nationalists and Loyalists together fought the army and police after a severe cut in Poor Law relief. The march itself when it reached London was attacked by the police, and when NUWM leader Wal Hannington was arrested, rioting took place throughout central London in protest.

NUWM organisation against the cuts continued with a further national march in early 1934; when it reached London, MacDonald as Prime Minister refused to receive a delegation, citing as precedent the actions of both the TUC and the Labour Party. Nevertheless, following a huge demonstration on 16 April, the Government was forced to restore the cuts of 1931, despite a declaration just beforehand that it saw no need to.

New regulations, to be introduced in early 1935 when there were still nearly two million unemployed, proposed a more stringent means test, and the establishment of 'training' or labour camps for those who were on transitional benefit having exhausted their 26 week entitlement. Once more it fell to the NUWM to campaign against them; the official labour movement had no response. The capacity of the NUWM to mobilise tens of thousands of people remained undiminished: 10,000 marched in North Shields, breaking a police ban; 300,000 in various parts of South Wales on Sunday 3 February. Cuts in transitional benefit were withdrawn as a result of the rising level of opposition.

The NUWM mobilised the unemployed and sections of the organised

---

31. Croucher, *op cit*, p132.

capable of representing their political interests. The Labour Party at each and every stage, along with the TUC, sought to isolate and destroy the NUWM, aided by the police and forces of the state. Many NUWM leaders served prison sentences as they stood with the unemployed. In contrast, Labour Party representatives co-operated in the administration of the means test; George Lansbury arguing at the 1932 conference that 'whilst it was true that when you are in a minority you cannot do much, you can do a little to soften the business' (ie administer the means test). [32] There was no practical challenge from the Labour left either: to take up the cause of the unemployed would have involved a break with the Party which was trying to crush their struggle.

The bitter hostility of the labour aristocracy towards the unemployed was all the more evident in their attitude to the 1936 Jarrow Crusade. This was the one march not organised by the NUWM: it was organised as a 'non-political' march, excluding known Communists, accepting every police rule, supported by the churches and both local Tory and Labour parties. Yet still Labour and the TUC circularised their local affiliates instructing them not to support the march or to provide it with any assistance, to the extent that in at least one place, where the local Labour Party and Trades Council refused to assist the march, it was the local Tory Party which organised food and accommodation.

Labour's response to the struggle of the unemployed has been often condemned but little understood. For instance, James Hinton has suggested that 'During the 1930s unemployed activism and local authority defiance of central government continued, but no effective way was found to direct this militancy into the national politics of the Labour Party' [33], whilst John Saville has described their opposition to Jarrow as the best example of Labour's 'stupid, reactionary and politically self-destructive' attitude in this period [34], and Miliband argued that 'Given the fact that Britain was in 1931 one of the richest

---

32. Quoted in Miliband, *op cit*, p212.
33. J Hinton, *Labour and Socialism – A History of the British Labour Movement 1867-1974*, Wheatsheaf, 1983, p135.
34. in ed A Briggs and J Saville, *Essays in Labour History 1918-39*, Croom Helm, 1977, p240.

countries in the world . . . it is surely amazing that there were actually found rational men to argue that the saving of a few million pounds a year on the miserable pittance allowed to unemployed men and women and their children was the essential condition of British solvency.'[35] Yet what else could have been the case? Maintaining the pre-1931 levels of unemployment benefit would have undermined the solvency of the most depressed industries which now absolutely depended on speed-up and wage cuts. The stagnant condition of the British economy meant that adequate conditions could not be sustained for the mass of the working class, but only for a minority. Resistance by the poorer sections merely threatened conditions for this affluent stratum, which Labour represented: militancy did not find its way into Labour politics because it was well and truly kept out, with the use of the police if necessary. Once again, none of these authors understand the political significance of a divided working class. Labour's attitude was certainly reactionary, but equally certainly not 'politically self-destructive' – after all, within ten years of the Jarrow march, it was to achieve a landslide parliamentary majority.

---

35. Miliband, *op cit*, p185.

Southall 1979: the black community protested against a National Front
election meeting and the police action to protect them. Anti-racist
demonstration. Blair Peach was murdered and 300 were arrested.

PART SIX

Labour and the working class from 1945

6.1 *Labour's 1945 electoral triumph*

The decisive factor in allowing Labour to obtain its huge parliamentary majority in 1945 was the vote of the middle class. In strongly working class constituencies, like Glasgow or Liverpool, the swing to Labour was 2.5 to 6.5 per cent, but in some of the South East constituencies, it was as high as 20 per cent. 'Over two million middle class voters had voted Labour, many for the first time.'[1] Birmingham, which had failed to return a single Labour MP in 1935, elected ten on an average swing of 23 per cent. In the counties, Labour took 110 seats as against the Tories' 112, but polled more votes: 4.6 million against 4.4 million.[2] A substantial section of the middle class had rejected the Tories.

This was in marked contrast with the previous election of 1935. Then Labour had captured 8.3 million votes and 154 seats; an improvement on the 6.6 million votes of 1931 with 52 seats, but still slightly below its 1929 vote, and well short of the 288 seats it had won at that election. Yet the recovery of 1935 was limited, and was explained partly by the increase in the overall electorate, and partly by increased support in the coalfields. In the prosperous South and Midlands, Labour made no headway. In the whole of the South of England outside London, the Government won 156 seats, Labour 15; inside London the figures were 39 and 22 respectively. In the Midlands, the seats divided three to

---

1. Morgan, *op cit*, p41.
2. A Sked and C Cook, *Post-War Britain: A Political History*, Harvester, 1979, p15.

one in favour of the Government, a figure nearly matched in the North-West. Labour failed to gain the votes of workers employed in the new industries and the service sector who lived in the southern part of the country who had had little contact with the means test or the PACs. Pointing out that a seat redistribution would benefit the Tories rather than Labour, the Coles argued that:

'As long as the suburbanites and the workers in the newer industries believe themselves to be tolerably secure in the conditions in which they are at present living, they will be in no mood for experiments which seem to them to threaten these conditions, however much the advocates of such experiments may hold out the prospect of a better society. They will vote predominantly for things as they are . . .'[3]

They concluded that only a war could alter this state of affairs and bring about conditions in which Labour would become electable, because: 'What most deeply imperils the British standard of living is the threat of war . . . .Under present conditions international politics are in reality the key to the domestic situation, for the prospects of the British people depend on what happens in international affairs. This is what the electors in the relatively comfortable areas must be made to see if they are to be detached from their present almost unreflective allegiance to things as they are.'[4]

This is in fact what happened. George Orwell, in his usual iconoclastic way, explained this in *The Lion and the Unicorn*, published in early 1941: 'People who at any other time would cling like glue to their miserable scraps of privilege, will surrender them fast enough when their country is in danger. War is the greatest of all agents of change. It speeds up all processes, wipes out minor distinctions, brings realities to the surface . . . If it can be made clear that defeating Hitler means wiping out class privilege, the great mass of middling people . . . will be on our

---

3. GDH and MI Cole, *The Condition of Britain*, Left Book Club, 1937, p421.
4. *ibid*, p423.

side.'[5] The legacy of appeasement, the incompetence that led to Dunkirk, the free rein given to left social democratic intellectuals to broadcast and write to recruit working class support for the war against fascism, all this had a significant impact on the middle class. On top of this was the Beveridge report and its treatment in the House of Commons. When it was published at the end of 1942, the response of the Coalition (in which Labour participated) was indifferent. During a debate on it in February 1943, Labour backbenchers forced a division on an amendment demanding immediate legislation. All the Parliamentary Labour Party outside the Government joined the rebellion, whilst the Tories opposed it. Tainted already by their support for appeasement, they were now seen to oppose Beveridge as well; for substantial sections of the middle class 'to believe in Beveridge was to have faith in a successful outcome to the war; more than that, it meant believing in a democratic distribution of the spoils of victory'.[6]

It took a world war to create an electoral constituency broad enough to return a majority Labour Government. This is important, because on only one other occasion has a Labour Government been elected with a substantial majority – in 1966. It shows that majority Labour Governments have only been elected in exceptional conditions, a fact that the left refuses to address. For instance, Ken Livingstone has argued that 'These bases of Labour's great success – led by Attlee in 1945 and Wilson in 1966 – came when we established a coalition between the highly-paid and skilled, and low-paid and unskilled sections of the working class electorate.'[7] This is undoubtedly true of 1945, but begs the question as to what were the preconditions for forging that coalition were. More recently, Paul Foot has suggested that 'The big Labour victories of 1945 and 1966 were won when the unions were strong, when nobody was out of work, and when the workers were full of confidence and hope.'[8] To ignore the political impact of six years of

---

5. Orwell, *op cit*, p102.
6. Sked and Cook, *op cit*, p20.
7. *Morning Star*, 28 April 1992.
8. *Socialist Review*, May 1992, p10.

world war and to ignore the significance of its outcome, with Britain not only a victor, but also without a European rival, displays complete fatuousness. Even then, as the Coles had pointed out, piling up the votes of the poor working class is not enough for a Labour victory: it must win the votes of the privileged strata and a significant section of the middle class as well; 1951 would prove this point once and for all.

6.2 The Post-War Labour Government

The composition of Labour MPs reflected the new-found radicalism of the middle class. Chuter Ede, later an extreme Conservative, pro-hanging Home Secretary, spoke of the Parliamentary Labour Party teeming 'with bright, vivacious servicemen. The superannuated Trade Union official seems hardly to be noticeable in the ranks.'[9] Despite the extensive middle class influence and activism within the Fabians and the ILP, the first Labour MP who might be described as middle class was not elected until 1922. In 1945, of 393 MPs, 119 were trade union sponsored as against 44 lawyers, 49 university lecturers, 25 journalists, 15 doctors and 18 company directors and businessmen.[10]

The Government set about its nationalisation proposals: the Bank of England – 'an essentially technical and institutional' change, and one which Churchill argued he could not oppose; Cable and Wireless – for 'the co-ordination of imperial cable and wireless services' – another one which the Tories could not oppose; the imperial factor enabled them to accede to the creation of BOAC and BEA without difficulty as well. These were followed by the creation of the Central Electricity Generating Board: 'Any opposition to the bill was mollified by the remarkably generous terms of compensation given to private stock-holders, whether company or individuals'[11], the nationalisation of gas and coal: Government policy was to defuse opposition by making concessions 'over compensation paid to private stockholders in coal,

---

9. Morgan, *op cit*, p59.
10. *ibid*, p60.
11. *ibid*, p103.

gas and electricity (which, in retrospect, seem almost inconceivably generous, especially in relation to coal).'[12]

The compensation for coal was indeed extraordinarily generous, the Government paying £164 million, and for the railways and canals, £1,000 million; these were industries which in the words of one commentator 'were badly run down, or badly organised, or underdeveloped and in need of new investment.'[13] In the process of nationalisation, Labour created the basis for the vast holding companies of today (BET, or British Electrical Traction, BTR, and the Hanson Trust from compensation paid out on coal nationalisation). Such industries could no longer be run on a privatised basis without severe rationalisation and consequent dislocation for the whole of British industry, as well as the creation of mass unemployment. Labour nationalised for the greater good of British capital as a whole, and to maintain full employment.

The Government also created the welfare state: the 1946 National Insurance and National Health Service Acts and the 1948 National Assistance Act being particular landmarks. More than this, the Government was able to preside over conditions of near full employment. From 1948, when industrial recovery really got under way, Britain was the only significant European industrial power; as Ian Aitken put it, 'Most of Europe was still in ruins, there were no dollars to buy American goods, and Britain's clapped-out factories were therefore able to sell everything they could produce.'[14] Although in the shadow of American imperialism, the world shortage of dollars meant that for a short period, British industry found little challenge, especially in its preferred Empire markets and within Europe itself. Unemployment in North East England, which had been 38 per cent in 1932, was 3 per cent in 1949; in industrial Scotland, the figure were 35 per cent and 4.5 per cent respectively, and South Wales, 41 per cent and 5.5 per cent. In Scotland, for instance, 536 factories were built through the Scottish

---

12. *ibid*, p109.
13. Brady, *Crisis in Britain*, 1950, quoted in Coates, *op cit*, p 53.
14. *The Guardian*, 1 June 1992.

Development Agency providing employment for 150,000. By 1951, overall unemployment was 1.8 per cent.

Whether or not real wages for the working class rose slightly, fell slightly or stayed the same, the fact remains that for large sections, real household income was much higher than prior to the war simply because they did not to have to support unemployed members of the family through the means test. The TUC leadership therefore experienced little pressure when it co-operated with the Government in controlling wage rises. If this failed, the Government had recourse to the 1920 Emergency Powers Act which it renewed in 1946, and proved perfectly willing to use troops – Aneurin Bevan as well as any – to break strikes, most notoriously during the April 1950 dockers' dispute. The end of mass unemployment was the key factor in sustaining a reasonably stable standard of living for masses of workers, far more than the welfare state itself. As Morgan notes:

> '. . . it was notorious that more affluent or middle class people received substantial help from universal welfare benefits. This especially applied to benefits in kind rather than cash, such as a free health service, free secondary school places, and food subsidies. The opportunities in health or education for the middle class (for instance, in the way they were able to benefit from the eleven plus examination through financial or cultural domestic advantage) enabled the gulf between them and manual workers to continue, if not grow even wider.' [15]

Despite this, Labour's parliamentary majority over the Tories was slashed in the 1950 General Election from 183 to 17, even though it polled 1.3 million more votes than in 1945. The South East had started to swing Tory especially in the London suburbs, more than cancelling out a small swing to Labour in South Wales and Scotland. As one commentator rather dramatically put it:

'Labour had frightened the middle classes in the suburbs of the

---

15. Morgan, *op cit*, p185.

home counties and the north as well, although it survived this loss of popularity because it could count on enthusiastic working class support.'[16]

Certainly it was the 92 mainly middle-class seats which had swung Conservative by over 7 per cent that really counted, rather than the 48 which had swung Labour. But it was not that the middle class had been frightened: more that they had returned to their natural home. The Tories had rid themselves of the stigma of appeasement, and had made clear their commitment to the welfare state. In the new-found conditions of economic progress, there was a middle-class rejection of the continuation of consumer controls, through rationing in particular.

The trend was accentuated in the 1951 Election: with the Liberals fielding only a little over 100 candidates, nearly two million of their votes went to the other two parties, dividing six to four in favour of the Tories.[17] 11 of the 21 Labour losses to the Tories were in London and the Home Counties. Thus it was that Labour, with a still larger vote than in 1950, and which still exceeded that of the Tories, found itself out of Government. Never before, and never since, had the working class voted so solidly for Labour: it may have lost the two million middle-class votes of 1945, but it had gained nearly four million votes from the working class. This, of course, is a point that both Livingstone and Foot, but particularly the latter, have difficulty in dealing with. Subsequent elections merely confirmed the trend of Labour dominant in the big towns, the North and South Wales; and the Conservatives in the South, the rural areas and the suburbs.

The 1945-51 Labour Governments had laid the basis of the post-war boom by firmly allying British imperialism to the might of US imperialism on the one hand, and making sure that the Empire paid for the costs of reconstruction on the other. As Bevin, echoing Churchill, had commented: 'I am not prepared to sacrifice the British Empire because I know that if the British Empire fell . . . it would mean the

---

16. Sked and Cook, *op cit*, p95.
17. Morgan, *op cit*, p486.

standard of life of our constituents would fall considerably.'[18] Hence the living standards of the British working class did not suffer during this period of reconstruction: the fruits of empire had been sufficient for British imperialism to make the necessary concessions domestically to ensure relative social peace. Even when in 1951 there was a massive increase in the balance of payment deficit as a result of the Korean war, the Government was able to allow the dollar surplus of the sterling area to take the strain: if the extra imports had to be paid for by extra exports, domestic consumption would have had to be cut by £350 million, not by the £50 million proposed.[19] Labour had delivered, but on the backs of the oppressed colonial people.

6.3   Labour and the boom

Despite the significant growth in industrial output under the Labour Government, and the relative increase in its contribution to the British imperialist economy, the tendency towards parasitism was never completely suppressed, and as the first signs of crisis appeared, re-asserted itself ever more strongly. British imperialism had not liquidated all its overseas assets during the war and 'net indebtedness was estimated to be very small in those early post-war years and was very soon made up by further foreign investment at a level unprecedented in absolute terms in British history . . . Britain made the transition from being a net debtor to being a net creditor in the early 1950s and has remained one ever since.'[20]

In 1948, Britain's share of world exports was more than twice that of France and Italy combined, at a time when the West German and Japanese economies were still scarcely functioning. Even as late as 1953, when the UK's share of world industrial output was 10 per cent, this compared favourably with the rest of the EEC countries at 16 per cent;

---

18. Quoted in R Palme Dutt, *The Crisis of Britain, op cit*, p80.
19. Gupta, *op cit*, p337.
20. G Phillips and R Maddock, *The Growth of the British Economy 1918-1968*, George Allen and Unwin, 1973, p139.

Japan's was a mere 2 per ecnt. Yet within ten years, the EEC share had risen to three times that of the UK and Japan almost matched it. By 1970, EEC output was over four times that of Britain, and Japanese output double. Underlying this were low domestic investment rates, and low increases in productivity when compared with its major competitors. This exposed the limits of reconstruction in the immediate post-war period: the temporary industrial ascendancy over its European rivals, coupled with the protection provided by monopoly control of imperial markets, meant that there was no immediate pressure to carry out significant rationalisation. More profitable investment could be found abroad, and that was where it went. Side by side with boom conditions went relative industrial decline; with relative decline came balance of payment problems, augmented by the continuing export of capital. These could be resolved only by periods of deflation: hence the so-called 'stop-go' economic policies of the 1950s and 1960s.

Although British growth was slower than that of its major competitors, it was more than sufficient to provide full employment; indeed, such was the demand for labour that British imperialism had to turn to external sources of supply. The dislocation at the end of the war provided for the first wave of immigrant labour: between 1945 and 1957, there was a net influx of 350,000 European nationals, together with a similar number of Irish workers. But as the European economies themselves expanded, this source dried up. Conveniently, another was at hand: the British colonies in Asia, Africa and the West Indies, where imperialist under-development had created a huge reserve army of labour. Immigration from these countries started in earnest at the beginning of the 1950s, and continued throughout the decade.

From the beginning, immigrant workers formed an oppressed section of the working class. They went into the lowest-paid jobs with the worst conditions, as white workers tended to move to better jobs, particularly in the service sector. Black workers were directed into NHS ancillary work and lower grade nursing jobs, and other menial public sector jobs, for instance in British Railways. The availability of this pool of labour helped maintain the viability of the welfare state, and thus proved an indirect benefit for the more privileged layers of the middle class.

Black workers were also extensively employed in the more backward sections of British manufacturing: in the small metal foundries of the Midlands and Sheffield, and in the textile mills of the North West where there was an extensive requirement for shift working; such patterns of work directed them also into the clothing sweat shops and the hotel and catering industry of London. The existence of this pool of labour enabled sections of British capital to extend the life-span of their assets, and therefore avoid the investment that would be needed to modernise the production process. In other words, immigrant labour was a substitute for investment. Thus, between 1961 and 1971, whereas employment in manufacturing fell overall by 745,000, the number of people employed in this sector who had been born outside of the UK *rose* by no less than 272,000.

By 1971, 71 per cent of black workers were concentrated in four major urban areas: Greater London, West Midlands, South East Lancashire and West Yorkshire, compared with 28 per cent of all economically active persons. For the age group 30-44, 43 per cent of all married women worked full-time, whereas the figure for those born in the New Commonwealth was 74 per cent. 50.6 per cent of all economically active males were manual workers; the figure for West Indian workers was 78.9 per cent, for Pakistanis 76.3 per cent, and for Indians 57.2 per cent. Shift working, which had greatly increased throughout the boom, was more prevalent among black workers: 15 per cent of white manual works were on shifts, compared with 31 per cent of black workers. Immigrant labour was overwhelmingly working class, concentrated in the worst jobs with the worst pay.

6.4 Labour in Government 1964-70

By the early 1960s, the extent of decline was making the successive balance of payment deficits ever more severe. It was clear that the Tories were incapable of overseeing the necessary changes to the industrial infrastructure, and that British capital needed a new approach. In 1964, Labour returned to office with a slender majority on a program of state-sponsored technological and economical development, to turn round the conditions which had contributed to Britain's industrial decline. They were confronted by the worst balance of payments deficit yet: £800 million. Labour met this with borrowings from the central banks and the IMF, together with a voluntary wage freeze and a mildly deflationary package in July 1965. Two months later, it published its National Plan, which envisaged nearly tripling annual investment rates, and increasing output by 25 per cent between 1964 and 1970.

Labour had won the 1964 Election not so much because it had gained support – in fact, it polled 12.2 million votes, virtually the same as in 1959 – but because a section of the middle class and privileged working class defected from the Tories to the Liberals. In the March 1966 Election, this section then moved to Labour, with the result that it was able to obtain a parliamentary majority of over 100. British imperialism could still afford to support the Keynesian consensus which enabled the mass of the working class to steadily increase its standard of living, and in 1966, both the privileged and less privileged layers of the working class voted Labour in sufficient numbers to give it its second largest majority ever. Yet these conditions were now drawing to a close, and the response of Labour was to attack its electoral base in the working class.

The first evidence of this was Prime Minister Harold Wilson's vitriolic attack on the striking seamen, including the claim that their action was being orchestrated by Communists. In July 1966, the Government announced a deflationary budget which included a legally binding wage freeze for six months, with a subsequent period of 'severe restraint'. A year later, the underlying trends had not improved; following adverse June trade figures, a run on the pound started, and continued throughout the autumn. Much as in 1949, Labour would not countenance devaluation until the last possible moment; attempts to defend the pound continued until 18 November, when the Government bowed to the inevitable and devalued the pound from $2.80 to $2.40. The Government secured credits of up to $3 billion, $1.4 billion from the IMF. Claims by Roy Jenkins, Chancellor of the Exchequer, that no strings were attached to the loans, and that there would be no need for a deflationary policy proved to be lies. In January 1968, Labour responded to demands that it cut domestic consumption by £750 million with an emergency budget. This deferred the raising of the school leaving age (from 15 to 16) from 1971 to 1973; it re-introduced prescription charges that had been abolished in 1965 and increased dental charges, and withdrew free school milk from secondary schools. That it also accelerated the withdrawal of British forces from East of Suez, and cancelled an order for F-111 fighter bombers was further recognition of its increasing inability to pursue an independent policing role for imperialism. The successive deflationary budgets made a nonsense of the National Plan; far from there being an increasing rate of domestic investment, it moved abroad at an accelerating pace.

A corollary of this process was a need for a reduced supply of immigrant labour. The first formal restrictions had been set out in the 1962 Commonwealth Immigrants Act, and were then supplemented by Labour's 1965 Act. The 1962 Act had introduced a voucher system to control the flow of immigrant labour: 'C' vouchers were for unskilled workers. The 1965 Act abolished 'C' vouchers, and imposed a limit of 8,500 on 'A' and 'B' vouchers (for skilled and professional workers), halving the numbers who had been admitted in 1964. The purpose, in the words of the Bill, was 'to control the entry of immigrants so that it does not outrun Britain's capacity to absorb them.' As Roy Hattersley said at the time to defend immigration controls, 'Without integration, limitation is inexcusable, without limitation, integration is impossible.'[21]

In 1968, as employment in manufacturing continued to decline, and unemployment started to rise, a further Act was introduced: the Commonwealth Immigration Act, which set forth the explicitly racist provision permitting entry only if the immigrant had a 'substantial connection' in Britain – that is, at least one grandparent. It also tore up the British passports of East African Asians and placed them within the same system of controls as other Commonwealth citizens. To this measure was added the 1969 Immigration Appeals Act. This shifted the

---

21. Quoted in M Williams, S Palmer and G Clapton, 'Racism, Imperialism and the Working Class', *Revolutionary Communist* No 9, 1979, p28. The material on racism is drawn from this article.

vetting of dependants from the port of entry to the country of departure. This made the process of proving a link between dependant and sponsor far more difficult, since it imposed a delay of many months, and was far more costly; in practice, it removed the right of admission to Britain from the husbands and fiancés of immigrants.

With the increasing economic difficulties came the first signs of political instability. From 1964 to 1970, the number of strikes more than doubled from 1,456 to 3,906; the number of days lost rose from 2.8 million in 1967 to 6.8 million in 1970. Many of the strikes were against the so-called 'productivity deals', or speed-ups, whereby British capital attempted to make existing assets more profitable rather than make new investments. In addition, there was the development of massive opposition to the Government's support for the US's war against Viet Nam, to be followed by the emergence of the Civil Rights campaign in the Six Counties. The unwillingness of the Government to take decisive action against the white settler state in Rhodesia contributed further to its loss of political credibility. The final straw was the introduction of the White Paper *In Place of Strife* in 1969, which sought to control the proliferation of unofficial strikes through statutory measures; the Government now viewed such industrial action as the biggest obstacle to the rationalisation of British industry. The opposition to it from amongst the trade union leadership was too great, however, and it was withdrawn ignominiously.

It was evident by 1970 that the Labour strategy had failed. Far from there being an increase in the rate of domestic investment, it had continued to fall along with the rate of profit. British capital needed a new strategy, one which sought the rationalisation of industry through closure of the most inefficient sections. The Tories 'lame ducks' policy appeared to meet this requirement, and in June 1970, they were elected with a substantial majority.

Yet Heath's strategy was to prove a complete fiasco. The Tories' own Industrial Relations Act was introduced against a background of serious opposition; their 'lame ducks' policy was blown off course by a prolonged 'work-in' at Upper Clyde Shipbuilders. A national coal strike in February 1972 was followed by a near-general strike in July when five dockers went to gaol in defiance of the Industrial Relations Act. In February 1974, as a second miners' strike plunged British industry into a three-day week, a change of government was essential to prevent complete chaos.

6.5   The deepening crisis: the 1974-79 Labour Government.

By the first 1974 Election, the position of the British imperialist economy was very weak. An inflationary boom artificially stimulated in 1972-73 had been followed by the Middle East war which drove up oil prices four-fold. A vast balance of payments deficit opened up, amounting to over £5 billion on visible trade, or over 6 per cent of GNP, and only partially offset by an invisible surplus. Inflation was running at 16 per cent in 1973-74 and 24.1 per cent in 1974-75. The response was a strongly deflationary budget for 1975 to reduce the Public Sector Borrowing Requirement (PSBR) to 8 per cent in 1975-76 and to 6 per cent in the following year. In addition to budgetary control, Labour introduced a wages policy in agreement with the TUC. The first stage imposed a ceiling on wage increases of £6 per week – some 10 per cent of average earnings, much less than the inflation rate.

Although this wages policy was hardly breached, it did not resolve any problems: the visible balance of payments deficit was still running at 3 per cent of GNP in 1975 and into 1976; by January, the pound had fallen to $2.04, and by the end of September to $1.64. Undaunted, the Government introduced the second stage of its income policy: from 1 August, increases were to be limited to 4.5 per cent, again in agreement with the TUC. The impact was later assessed by *The Economist*:

' . . . the 7 per cent by which the past year's 10 per cent increase in earnings fell behind its 17 per cent increase in prices represents the biggest recorded fall in the average Briton's real disposable income for over a hundred years: worse than anything that happened in the 1930s.'[22]

---

22. Quoted in Editorial, *Revolutionary Communist* No 7, 1977, p1.

In December 1975, the Government approached the IMF for its first loan to support the pound. With the PSBR still out of control, substantial cuts in public spending were announced in February (£2 billion; £600 million from education alone) and further cuts in July (£1 billion). The run on the pound continued: in the two months to April, the Government had used $2.75 billion supporting it, and had exhausted the IMF loan. By autumn, with no fundamental change in the situation, and with the central banks refusing to bail it out, the Government turned once more to the IMF. In return for a further loan of $3.9 billion, it agreed to impose cuts of £3 billion in public spending over a period of two years. In actual fact, state spending was to fall much further: from 49.35 per cent of GDP in 1975-76 to 43.25 per cent in 1977-78 before recovering slightly to 44 per cent in 1978-79. In real terms, it fell from £195.3 billion in 1975-76 to £181.1 billion in 1977-78, recovering to £190.1 billion in 1978-79; a feat 13 years of Tory rule could never achieve.

It was also during this period that the more parasitic features of British imperialism started to come to the fore, as the London Eurocurrency market became a central source of loan capital throughout the world. Between 1972 and 1979, Eurocurrency bank credits grew from $7 billion to $83; of these, $2.5 and $48 billion respectively were to oppressed nations; 30 per cent of this was accounted for by the City of London. Direct investment, though on a much smaller scale, proved extremely profitable: between 1972 and 1977, the rate of profit on such investment in the oppressed nations averaged 18-20 per cent, compared to 3.6 to 4.2 per cent for domestic industry. Overall, the private external assets of British imperialism grew from £61 billion in 1973 to £119 billion in 1977; in 1962, such assets had made up some 40 per cent of GNP; in 1977, they had risen to 93 per cent. The seeds of the debt crisis of the oppressed nations were sown in this period, as British imperialism utilised its dominant position in the financial services market to shore up its domestic position. This was taking place exactly at the same time as Tony Benn was claiming that 'Britain had moved from Empire to colony status', arguing that Britain 'is a colony in which the IMF decides our monetary policy, the international and multinational companies decided our industrial policy, and the EEC decides our legislative and taxation policy.'[23]

A further stage in the wages policy was imposed in 1977, this time without TUC agreement, followed by a fourth stage in August 1978. But the strain for wide sections of the working class was too much, especially in the public sector where such policies could be more effectively imposed, and as unemployment rose by a million. The result was the Winter of Discontent, as low-paid council workers came out on strike in an attempt to restore their living standards. The social-democratic consensus had truly broken down.

Although the mass of the working class suffered increasing hardship under the Labour Government, black workers experienced even greater oppression. Thus Labour continued to operate the 1971 Immigration Act despite its earlier declarations of opposition. This Act essentially introduced a work permit system: there were to be no more immigrants, only 'guest workers'. As a corollary, there would be no secondary immigration associated with such migrant workers, and such secondary immigration as did take place of dependants of black workers already settled in Britain was made brutally oppressive. The Act greatly increased powers of deportation, to the extent that on average there were over 200 black people awaiting deportation each day. This Act facilitated the use of X-ray examinations to disprove childrens' age claims, and the use of virginity testing. In 1977, it was tightened even further when a 12 month probation period was put on the marriages of immigrant husbands after extensive publicity about alleged 'marriages of convenience'.

This was not the end of Labour's attacks on the black working class. It used thousands of police to defeat the Grunwick's strike of Asian women in 1976, and sanctioned the attack on the Notting Hill Carnival of 1976. It tolerated the ever-extending use by the police of the 1824 Vagrancy Act – the 'sus' law – which enabled them to constantly harass black youth. Not even refugees were exempt from Labour's attentions

---

23. Quoted in M Williams, S Palmer and G Clapton, *op cit*, *Revolutionary Communist* No 9, p3.

in 1974–75: Cypriot refugees from the civil war were denied entry, as were Rhodesian draft-dodgers in 1976–77. The Prevention of Terrorism Act was introduced in December 1974 to repress the Irish.

Given the presence of significant numbers of black and Irish workers in the state sector, the political consequences were to be significant. Irish people, traditionally Labour supporters when in Britain, had turned against it as a result of its policies of torture and criminalisation in the Six Counties. Black people started organising against racism: Asian Youth Movements emerged, as well as a variety of ad-hoc committees to defend victims of state oppression. In November 1979, 20,000 Asian workers were to demonstrate against the immigration laws, cheering speakers who denounced Labour's racism. A year beforehand, a motion calling on NUPE to disaffiliate from the Labour Party had been debated at its annual conference. In defending their political interests, black and Irish workers were having to confront the Labour Party. Labour's agreement during the 1979 General Election campaign to use thousands of police to defend a National Front election rally in Southall merely drove the point home. 300 people were arrested, and Blair Peach was killed as the police fought a pitched battle with the youth. In the June 1979 Election, thousands of black and Irish people, once the most committed Labour voters, abstained from voting at all.

6.6   *Labour and the working class under the Tories*

Although substantial numbers of poorer workers abstained in 1979, the principal factor in the Tories' victory was the defection of sections of the more privileged sections of the working class, especially in the South East. Labour's share of the votes of trade unionists fell from 66 per cent in 1970 to 55 per cent in 1974, and 51 per cent in 1979. In 1974, 49 per cent of the so-called C2 voters (skilled workers, foremen and the self-employed) voted Labour, enabling it to just scrape home. In 1979, the largest swing against Labour was from within this stratum – over 10 per cent. The division within the working class was now becoming evident at the electoral level.

Underlying this were major changes within the structure of the working class, with a major shift in employment from the productive, manufacturing sector to the service sector (Table 9).

Within the manufacturing sector, the pattern of employment had also changed, as the number of white collar workers increased at the same time as the number of manual workers declined (Table 10).

The number of miners, railwaymen and manual workers in manufacturing – in other words, the core of traditional Labour voters – numbered 8.13 million in 1948, 7.76 million in 1964, and only 5.52 million in 1979. The number of those employed in banking, finance, insurance and professional services had risen from 1.74 million to 2.94

Table 9 **Employment Changes 1948-79** (000s) [24]

Employment Category	1948	1958	1964	1968	1972	1979
Coal Mining	802	785	596	446	330	300
Manufacturing	8035	8932	8796	8797	7613	7107
Railways	578	494	394	298	241	183
Distributive Trades	2033	2493	2962	2828	2587	3001
Banking, Finance & Insurance	434	501	627	674	983	1621
Professional Services (Inc Teaching & Health)	1306	1786	2310	2702	3030	3432
Public Administration	1445	1283	1389	1507	1513	1668
Misc Services	1827	1598	2185	2148	2001	2037

Table 10 **Employment in Manufacturing 1948-79** (000s) [25]

	1948	1958	1964	1973	1979
1 Total No Employees	8035	8932	8797	8048	7055
2 Manual Workers	6749	7038	6768	5876	5040
3 Admin, Technical and Clerical Staff	1286	1894	2029	2172	2015
3 as a percentage of 1	16.0	21.2	23.1	27.0	28.6

24. Drawn from various issues of the *Ministry of Labour* and *Department of Employment Gazettes*.
25. *ibid.*

million and then 5.05 million over the same period. The rate of change in employment patterns was far more rapid between 1964 and 1979, the years of deepening crisis, than it had been between 1948 and 1964. The privileged stratum of the working class still existed – it had however taken on a different form: skilled workers were now white collar employees, without the same commitment to Labour as their manual predecessors. The tendencies noted by the Coles in the 1930s were now a reality; to survive as a party, Labour would have to appeal to this new labour aristocracy.

The Tories had been elected on the strength of their commitment to cut public sector expenditure, attack working class living standards and thereby halt Britain's economic decline whilst sustaining its role as a major imperialist power. The first fruit of this shift in strategy was the slump of 1980-81, when unemployment rose beyond three million and employment in manufacturing fell from seven million to six million. Resistance proved scant; a 14-week strike by steel-workers in British Steel was defeated as steel continued to pour out of foundries in the private sector.

The response of Labour to their losing the Election was to adopt a series of radical policies. But the apparent ascendancy of the left was in sharp contrast to the increasing separation of the Party from the mass of the working class. The left's victories at successive Conferences had more to do with the internal administration of the Party than with anything else. The response to the uprisings during the summer of that year was a case in point. Labour, left or right, had no sympathy for the youth both black and white who fought police oppression and racism. Thus Michael Foot told the 1981 Labour Party Conference that 'what happened in Moss Side and Liverpool is what we in the Labour Party are dedicated to stop'[26], whilst Tony Benn was of the opinion that 'the Labour Party does not believe in rioting as a route to social progress nor are we prepared to see the police injured during the course of their duties.'[27] This attack was reinforced by the left as it

26. Quoted in article by S Palmer, *Fight Racism! Fight Imperialism!* No 13, October 1981.
27. Quoted in Editorial, *Fight Racism! Fight Imperialism!* No 12, September 1981.

protected the open racists within the Labour Party, the SWP, for instance, describing black youth as a 'lumpen proletariat', a 'vulnerable underbelly of the working class'.[28] No matter how reactionary the Labour Party became, it would still have its defenders to the left, prepared to reconcile their support for Labour with anything and everything. In the absence of any movement which could represent their political interests, the youth were isolated, and no organisational legacy of their struggle emerged.

The same summer had witnessed the valiant hunger strike of Irish political prisoners, and the deaths of ten of them. As we have seen, Labour supported the Tories fully throughout the strike; not one MP expressed any support for them publicly. But it was the radical and socialist phrases which mattered to many on the left, who entered Labour in significant numbers from the Communist Party and various Trotskyist groups during these years. After all, if the SWP's Paul Foot could argue from outside the Labour Party: 'There can hardly have been a socialist in Britain who did not feel warmth and solidarity for Tony Benn', just after he had kept his mouth firmly shut during the 1980 Labour Conference debate on political status for Irish political prisoners, the culture of corruption was spreading far and wide.

If Labour was no longer in office, it was of course still a major force in local government. Hence municipal socialism became an avenue through which Labour sought to appeal to the new labour aristocracy of the public sector, and a particularly corrupt one at that. Many were the jobs and especially non-jobs that were given to graduates, as the left feathered its own nest. Spurious community groups, housing schemes, race relation units for a tiny privileged layer of black and Irish people, all were designed to bring the maximum personal benefit to those who found jobs and funding through them, and the minimum of benefit to those who were really suffering the onslaught of Thatcherism. The Fare's Fair dispute of 1982 showed the real limits of municipal socialism at an early stage, when the Law Lords overruled an attempt to establish

---

28. Quoted in Editorial, *Fight Racism! Fight Imperialism!* No 14, November 1981.

reasonable fares for London Transport, and Ken Livingstone's Greater London Council decided not to make a fight of it.

It was not just municipal socialism that was shown to be impotent in 1982: so was the trade union movement in two disputes. In the first, ASLEF and the NUR first engaged in a slanging match, and then refused to co-ordinate any joint campaign over a pay claim against British Rail. Later in the year, a pay claim by nurses and ancillary workers was allowed to drag on without any resolution for seven months, with the TUC refusing to organise any support. The depth of the crisis was now such that the trade union methods of ten years before were no longer a feasible means of defending the working class. In the early 1970s, there had still been some basis for unity between the privileged sections and the mass of the working class, the precondition for legal trade unionism. But the decline of British imperialism now meant that it could only maintain existing conditions for the upper stratum of the working class, and this stratum became more and more willing to scab on the rest of the working class whenever the latter sought to defend itself in action. The 1984/85 miners' strike would drive this point home.

The widening division in the working class became evident in election results during 1982 and 1983. In February 1982 Peter Tatchell was defeated in what had been Labour's sixth safest seat, Bermondsey, in a clear example of anti-gay prejudice. This was followed by the débâcle of the 1983 General Election, when Labour lost three million votes compared to its 1979 result, and polled only 28 per cent of the vote. The election was marked by increasing levels of abstention in the poor, inner-city constituencies – a poll indicated that only 33 per cent of black people were going to vote – and the continued defection of the privileged strata of the working class – only 34 per cent of C2 voters supported Labour. The first rounds of privatisation, and the sale of council houses in particular had started to give this section of the working class a substantial stake in the system. No less than 59 per cent of 1979 Labour voters who bought their council houses between 1979 and 1983 switched their vote at the second election. Since 1979, whereas skilled workers had at worst held their own, the unskilled and semi-skilled had on average suffered a fall of 4-8 per cent in real wages.

The self-satisfaction of the better-off stratum expressed itself then in an increasing conservatism, and an increased hostility to any action which might threaten their conditions. The TUC responded to this with the policy of New Realism, of avoiding struggle at all costs, whilst Labour responded with the election of Neil Kinnock as its leader as part of the 'dream ticket' with Roy Hattersley. During his leadership campaign, Kinnock made clear the constituency to which he would appeal:

> ' ... we can only protect the disadvantaged in our society if we appeal to those who are relatively advantaged. The apparent over-concentration of our energies and resources on these groups like the poor, the unemployed and the minorities – does a disservice both to them and to ourselves ... if we are to be of real use to the deprived and insecure we must have the support of those in more secure social circumstances – the home owners as well as the homeless, the stable family as well as the single parent, the confidently employed as well as the unemployed, the majority as well as the minorities.'[29]

In other words, a future Labour victory would depend on its ability to appeal to the privileged. This was a rebuttal of those like Livingstone who had argued that Labour had to appeal to precisely these groups 'like the poor, the unemployed and the minorities', in contrast to electricians and engineers whom he described as 'privileged "labour aristocrats" ', and white collar workers who were 'middle class'. Once again, it was up to the left to come to the defence of privilege; thus Alex Callinicos from the SWP argued:

> 'One wonders who is left in the working class according to Livingstone. The implication of this sort of analysis is that socialists must create a new popular base by linking up with groups which are not part of the working class. The examples most often given are those of such "minorities" as women, blacks and gays.'[30]

---

29. Quoted in Editorial, *Fight Racism! Fight Imperialism!* No 33, October 1983.
30. Quoted *ibid.*

Already implicit in this is the notion of the 'underclass': that the working class is equivalent to the trade union movement, and any poor person who is not in a trade union is outside of the working class. This notion was familiar to the old craft unionists, to Sidney Webb when he wrote his London Programme, to those who opposed the movement of the unemployed between the wars. It is a view that stamps its protagonists as defenders of privilege, since they argue that it is the upper stratum of the working class that will be the agency of social change, much as the Webbs thought the professional middle class would be. Just how privileged the average Labour Party member is was revealed in a report by Larry Whitty in 1987:

> '60 per cent of party members have a degree or equivalent higher educational qualification, compared to a national average of just 11 per cent. Labour Party members are twice as likely to be employed in the public sector as the private. 62 per cent of them read *The Guardian*, and only 25 per cent the *Daily Mirror*.'[31]

Following 1983, Kinnock consistently pursued the interests of privileged sections of the working class and its middle class allies. The year after his election he was attacking councils which refused to set a legal rate: they 'would do best . . . to stay in the positions to which they have been elected so that they can mitigate, protect and dilute the effect of central government planning'[32], an echo of George Lansbury's appeal 50 years earlier for Labour authorities to implement the means test. By 1985, any resistance to rate-capping had collapsed.

But the decisive battle was the 1984/85 miners' strike, where the divisions evident in the strikes of the early 1980s came to the fore. The relatively greater security and better conditions of the Nottinghamshire miners first made them indifferent to the plight of those communities which were under threat in Scotland, Yorkshire and Wales, then hostile, as they went through picket lines, and finally, willing tools in the effort of British Coal to break the strike. There were other differences, too. In

---

31. Quoted in Cliff and Gluckstein, *op cit*, p351.
32. Quoted in article by R Clough, *Fight Racism! Fight Imperialism!* No 39, May 1984.

Arthur Scargill, the miners had a leader who probably came as close to a revolutionary trade unionist standpoint as was possible, and who was willing to stand by them when they were attacked by the police and by the media. They were also ready to accept new methods of organisation: in particular, the support groups set up by miners' wives which sought to harness support from within the communities. Yet the strike was defeated, not just by the state, but also by the forces of the trade union movement and the Labour Party, who successfully isolated the miners and the section of the working class that supported them.

The process, which started with the refusal of Nottingham miners to support the strike call, continued when TUC General Secretary Len Murray declared one-day strikes in Yorkshire and Wales on 20 May 1984 'unconstitutional', and instructed union leaders to call them off. Tony Benn withdrew a motion to the Labour Party National Executive calling for national demonstrations in favour of a far vaguer motion which committed Labour to nothing. The Iron and Steel Trades Confederation (ISTC) members, egged on by Bill Sirs, helped non-union labour unload a shipload of coal at Hunterston – enough to keep the Ravenscraig plant going for several weeks. As BSC stepped up imports of coal, there were attempts to get dockers not to handle such cargoes. Yet whilst most Dock Labour Scheme ports came out, unregistered dockers did not; as a Great Yarmouth T&GWU branch secretary said:

> 'We have helped the miners in the past with money but we draw a line at this. The talk about scab labour is just an excuse. We shall work and we shall cross picket lines if we have to.'[33]

The dockers' support petered out. The scabbing continued: at the September TUC Congress, Neil Kinnock denounced the miners for defending themselves:

> 'violence, I do not have to tell this Congress ... disgusts union

---

33. Quoted in D Reed and O Adamson, *The Miners' Strike 1984-85 – People versus State*, Larkin, 1985, p45.

opinion and divides union attitudes . . . and is alien to the tempera-
ment and intelligence of the British trade union movement.'[34]

Power workers in the Electrical Engineers' and Plumbers Trade Union
(EEPTU) voted by 84 per cent not to support the miners on 19 October.
On 24 October, the colliery officials' union, NACODS, called off its
strike after the Coal Board changed colliery review procedures. On 3
November, Kinnock announced that he was 'too busy' to attend any
NUM rallies. Meanwhile, the TUC put intense pressure on the NUM to
surrender. Yet the miners held out for a further four months in their
desperate attempt to defend their communities before finally being
forced back to work.

The official trade union movement and the Labour Party had sided
with the privileged section of the working class – the Nottingham
miners, the colliery inspectors, the non-registered dockers. Whilst
police had besieged and terrorised mining communities, placed them
under curfew, set up road blocks hundreds of miles away from any
picket line, offered any amount of protection to scabs, arrested and
beaten hundreds of miners, the official labour movement had denounced the miners when they attempted to defend themselves. It was
not just the leaders – it was their erstwhile left-wing critics as well.
Hence *Socialist Worker* denounced miners' hit squads by saying 'such
raids can give trade union officials an excuse not to deliver solidarity',
and more generally argued 'we are opposed to individuals or groups
using violence as a substitute for mass struggle. That's why we oppose
planting bombs, assassinating politicians and criticise some of the
miners' hit squads.'[35] NUM leaders, Scargill in particular, were made of
different stuff from the SWP, and did not join in these cowardly attacks.

Cliff and Gluckstein go further in their attack on the conduct of the
strike, and argue that compared to 1972, 'Rank and file activity was
lower, and crucially, the miners showed less willingness to act

---

34. *ibid*, p51.
35. *Socialist Worker*, 11 and 25 August 1984, quoted *ibid*, p45.

independently of the bureaucracy'.[36] They argue, in defence of the privileged section of the working class, that the reason that sections such as power workers and engineers did not take action in support of the miners is that they 'lacked confidence'. Both here and over the issue of violence, the SWP, in common with the bulk of the left, put the interests of the upper stratum of the working class before that of the majority. As after the 1981 uprisings, a section of the working class driven into action had found no political force to represent its interests.

6.7   The impact of Thatcherism on the working class

Throughout the 1980s, Thatcher was able to dramatically accelerate the changes in the social and political character of the British working class that had started with the onset of the crisis (Table 11).

The number of manual workers employed in manufacturing fell from 5,040,000 to 3,294,000; adding the 206,000 railwaymen and coal miners gives a total of 3,500,000 compared with the 5,520,000 thus employed in June 1979, or the 7,758,000 of 1964. In complete contrast, the numbers employed in Banking, Finance, Insurance and Professional Services rose from 3,699,000 in 1964 to 5,053,000 in 1979 and

Table 11   **Employment Changes 1979-1991**   (000s) [37]

	1979	1991
Coal Mining	300	74
Manufacturing	7107	4642
Railways	183	132
Distributive Trades	3001	3171
Banking, Finance, Insurance	1621	2616
Professional Services	3432	4124
Public Administration	1668	1571
Miscellaneous Services	2037	2096

36. Cliff and Gluckstein, *op cit*, p347.
37. Drawn from various issues of the *Employment Gazette*.

6,740,000 in 1991. In addition to this, the number of self-employed rose from 1,842,000 in 1979 to 3,222,000 in 1991. Trade union membership fell from over 12 million to just over eight million over the same period.

Meanwhile, owner-occupation increased from roughly 53 per cent to nearly 67 per cent in 1991 – 15.7 million people now own their own homes. Council housing stock fell from 6.5 million to about five million as more than a million tenants exercised their right to buy. The number of outstanding mortgages rose by 60 per cent, from 6.2 million in 1980 to 9.8 million in 1991. In 1990, one in four of the adult population were shareholders compared with one in 13 in 1991. Through privatisation, home ownership and so-called 'people's capitalism', Thatcher destroyed the old social base for the Labour Party and gave a substantial section of the working and lower middle class a material stake in the system.

Parallel to this process, the gap between rich and poor significantly widened. The real income of the poorest 20 per cent of the population fell from £3,442 per annum to £3,282 between 1979 and 1989 at constant prices. That of the top 20 per cent increased from £20,138 to £28,124: from six times the income of the poorest 20 per cent to nearly nine times. Income tax cuts worth nearly £29 billion were made between 1979 and 1991, the chief beneficiaries being the rich, the middle class and the better-off workers. In 1979, there were 7.8 million workers earning less than the Council of Europe's decency threshold. Today the figure is ten million – 47 per cent of all employees. The gap between the highest and lowest paid male manual worker is greater than in Victorian times. 10.3 million people including 2.6 million children live in poverty. By 1987, more than a third of the UK population were living in poverty or on its margins, up 50 per cent on 1979. Changes in the social security system were key factors in this rise.

However, it is the middle class and better-off sections of the working class who determine the outcome of elections, and if Labour was to recover their support, it had to adapt to their prejudices. The defeat of the miners removed any obstacle to this process. In 1986, it approved the sale of council properties, whilst in the following year, Bryan Gould was able to argue that 'The idea of owning shares is catching on, and as socialists, we should support it as one means of taking power from the hands of the few and spreading it more widely.' Unilateralism was also under attack, even if indirectly: in 1984, Kinnock had gone to the US to assure the American allies that Labour was 'neither cowardly, complacent nor pacifist', and that position was overwhelmingly endorsed in 1986 when the Conference voted five to one to remain in NATO. The next January, when the *Secret Society* TV programme was banned because it would reveal the fact that a £500 million spy-satellite project had been kept secret from Parliament, Kinnock stated 'I would have done the same. The Government are right to seek to take the action to prevent publication, wrong to fail to ensure all the angles were covered' – referring to the fact that the details had got out in the *New Statesman* because of Government incompetence.

By this time, Labour had dropped any pretence of defending the poorer sections of the working class. It was left to charities or churches to express any concern, as the latter did with the publication of *Faith in the Inner Cities*. As if to underline this, Labour Chairperson Tom Sawyer urged the Party in the lead-up to the General Election 'not to write off the white, heterosexual working class and replace them with a coalition of the dispossessed'. When the Election came, however, the economy appeared to be booming: 1986 had seen Britain become the largest creditor nation (net overseas assets over £100 billion) as the City of London remained the financial centre of the world; annual growth was over four per cent; the Government account was in surplus; unemployment was falling and house prices booming. In such circumstance, it was not surprising that the better-off sections of the working class continued to place their faith in the Tories, and returned them with yet another large majority.

6.8 *To the 1992 General Election*

In 1989, Labour became a 'fair tax party', accepting a maximum rate of 50 per cent. Meanwhile, it made clear it would oppose any campaign of non-payment of the Poll Tax, a position which was passed overwhelmingly at a Recall Conference of the Scottish Labour Party in

September 1988. The result was a heavy defeat in the Govan by-election in November 1988, when there was a 33 per cent swing to the SNP. Kinnock had earlier described such a campaign as a 'counsel of despair, fruitless'. Meanwhile, Margaret Hodge, Labour leader of Islington Council in London, claimed a 'victory' in 'forcing' the Government to introduce the tax in one go in England rather than phase it in as was originally proposed. This, said Hodge, 'removes an unnecessary administrative burden.' – but it also meant that the working class would have to pay more immediately. Hence administrative convenience assumed greater importance for the privileged than the poverty of the less well-off sections of the working class. The movement against the Poll Tax, however, remained committed to the Labour Party, whether it was led by the Militant or by the SWP. And, as if to echo Labour's contempt for the poor, a leading member of the SWP, Chris Harman, argued at the 1988 Socialist Conference that it was not possible to build a community-based campaign against the tax because 'On council estates are drug peddlers, junkies and people claiming houses under false names. These people will complete the registration forms to avoid attention from the council', [38] and went on to argue that the central issue was the Benn-Heffer leadership campaign. Sidney Webb would have approved.

The only occasions on which Labour leaders felt the urge to deal with issues facing the poorer sections of the working class was when they offered any resistance to their lot. The 1989 uprising at Risley Remand Centre caused Hattersley to exclaim 'No-one should defend the violence at Risley or react in a way which might incite similar action in other prisons' [39] – although a jury was later to accept that the actions of the prisoners were justifiable self-defence. Hattersley was to make the same noises during the Strangeways uprising the following year, calling for forcible tactics to be used against the prisoners, which in local Labour MP Bob Litherland's words became a call on the Home Office

---

38. Quoted in D Reed and L Reid, *Fight Racism! Fight Imperialism!* No 79, July 1988.
39. Quoted in A Byrne, *Fight Racism! Fight Imperialism!* No 87, June 1989.

'to intervene and arrange for the SAS to take over.'[40] Hattersley was equally in his element in dealing with the Poll Tax riot: 'I hope there have been a substantial number of arrests, and that the sentencing is severe . . . exemplary.'[41] Strong stuff indeed for a Party which professes an abhorrence for violence, yet essential if it were to win the allegiance of semi-detached Britain.

Meanwhile, the decay of municipal socialism went on apace, as Labour councils started to implement severe cuts in the wake of the Poll Tax. Newcastle Council cut 1,000 jobs as it reduced spending by £17.5 million, Coventry nearly 300 jobs; Manchester Council cut 10 per cent of its workforce over a four-year period, Lothian refused to fill 600 vacancies in social services. In London, Camden cut £30 million in its 1991/92 budget, despite raising rents by £17 per week; Greenwich cut 450 jobs, Newham 340 jobs in education and social services. Reductions in services were universal, as the poorer sections of the working class suffered doubly: having to pay more, and getting far less in return.

Labour went into the 1992 Election almost indistinguishable on major policy issues from the Tory Party it professed to oppose. It had not only renounced unilateralism, but refused to say whether it would cancel the fourth Trident submarine. It made no commitment to restore any of the under-funding of the state sector, beyond spending an extra £1 billion on the NHS over a period of 22 months and £600 million on education, sufficient it felt to maintain the electoral support of the poorer sections of the working class. It was committed to the EC, to the Exchange Rate Mechanism, and strenuously opposed any devaluation of the pound. It would not revoke the fundamentals of the Tory trade union laws, nor amend any immigration laws. It would increase pensions – but only by £5 out of the £14 that had been lost since pension increases were no longer indexed to pay increases; it also promised to restore the cuts in child benefit. It emphasised that although it would raise the top level of taxation to 50 per cent, this would only affect those earning £38,000 or more. It also proposed to abolish the

---

40. Quoted in L Reid, *Fight Racism! Fight Imperialism!* No 94, April 1990.
41. Quoted *ibid*.

ceiling on National Insurance contributions, currently standing at just over £20,000, to provide sufficient funds for the very modest extra public spending which would hardly begin to address the poverty created by years of Tory rule.

In the end, even these proved too much for wide sections of the middle class and better-off workers to accept. Where Labour gained, it did so almost entirely at the expense of the Liberal Democrats, whose proposals for extra taxation were both more extensive and more frankly argued. Labour recovered support from skilled workers – just over 40 per cent voted for them in 1992 according to both Mori and NOP as opposed to 35 per cent in 1987.[42] Yet this only took them back to the 1979 position, and was far short of the 49 per cent who had voted for them in 1974. Amongst middle class trade unionists (a pollsters' term for better-off white collar trade unionists), it increased its support from 30 per cent to 36 per cent – but this just brought it up to the level of Conservative support; overall, the middle class (C1) divided 52 per cent to 24 per cent in favour of the Tories. Its bare majority amongst working class trade unionists (51 per cent in 1987) was only slightly up, at 55 per cent. More significantly, it still had less support than the Tories amongst working class owner-occupiers (39 per cent against 41 per cent), whilst support amongst council tenants slipped slightly (59 per cent to 58 per cent).

In the South, the Tories still predominated, with 51 per cent of the vote outside of London as against 24 per cent for Labour, a voting pattern which translated into 106 Tory seats as opposed to three Labour. In London itself, the gap, although closer (12 per cent) than in 1987 (18 per cent) was still enough to give 46 per cent of the vote to the Tories and a substantial majority of seats. The middle class and the more affluent sections of the working class felt that their interests were still safer with the Tories.

The inquest into the General Election started immediately. Ken Livingstone argued the next day that: 'We must be able to build socialism

---

42. Figures in this and the subsequent paragraph are drawn from *The Times*, 11 April 1992; and *The Independent on Sunday*, 12 April 1992.

without taxing middle income families till it hurts', and continued: 'If you analyse the result I suspect that we just failed to win seats we should have because people on middle incomes were concerned. In London and the South East, £21,000 is average earnings and should not have been a target for higher tax. I have always argued the figure should have been £26,000.'[43] All this was a far cry from his 1983 'coalition of the dispossessed'. Others on the left echoed his view. Militant thought that 'starting tax rises at £21,000 a year could give the Tories ammunition. The tax issue could still make the difference with better-paid skilled and white-collar workers – vital votes Labour has to win back'[44], whilst, according to its post-mortem, 'white-collar workers, middle ranking teachers and middle class voters who could be won to Labour' were not, because they 'got the impression Labour would tax them harder', and it referred editorially to the 'tax disaster'. This was in fact the only equitable proposal that Labour put forward during the election, and shows how much the left was prepared to concede to get Labour re-elected.

Another view was expressed by Dennis Skinner, who complained of listening to the SDP and Liberal Democrats 'about how we should collaborate and accept their policies' and stated that: 'it is time we represented our class. We don't need the Liberals and proportional representation to do that. What we need is class politics.'[45] But Labour had proscribed, expelled, and attacked anything that smacked of working class politics during the 1980s, and Skinner did not suggest what forces exist to make it carry out such a *volte-face*. This view again had a left-wing echo, when the SWP suggested that Labour lost because it 'turned its back on working class struggles': this did not prevent it from urging support for Labour, and describing its defeat as a 'disaster'.[46]

---

43. *Evening Standard*, 10 April 1992.
44. *Militant*, 20 March 1992.
45. *The Independent*, 11 April 1992.
46. *Socialist Worker*, 18 April 1992. Luxemburg's description of German Social Democracy as a 'stinking corpse' is pertinent here. There is no reason to suppose she thought any different of British social democracy, so it is somewhat surprising to be told by those who are so fond of the great revolutionary that the failure to elect this 'stinking corpse' is in fact a major 'disaster'. Unless of course they believe in re-incarnation . . .

The SWP also echoed Labour's concern for the moral well-being of the more affluent sections of the working class, and in particular showed determination to scotch 'the myth that it was the C2s, the better-paid skilled workers, especially in the South East, who cost Labour the election.'[47] As we have seen, it may have got 43 per cent of the C2 vote in 1992, but it needed 49 per cent in 1974 in order to just scrape home, and we have also shown the effect that purchasing a council house had on voting patterns in 1983. To attempt to bolster this position, they have argued that the C2 layer is made up of the self-employed and foremen as well as 'genuine' skilled workers, and that these 'genuine' skilled workers always vote Labour. But the distinction the SWP draws between skilled workers as employees and skilled workers as the self-employed (the collapse of manufacturing employment has made the foreman category far less significant) serves only to hide how this layer as a whole has benefitted from the Tories' 'people's capitalism'. The number of self-employed rose by nearly 1.5 million during the Tory years, many being skilled workers investing their redundancy pay.

Although the left talked about class politics, their primary concern was with one, minority section of the working class. They merely provide a radical interpretation of the standpoint of the Labour leadership. Thus John Smith, commenting on JK Galbraith's book *The Culture of Contentment*, which argues that the basis for the post-war consensus has now completely disappeared, says that: 'I do not accept that his pessimism is warranted in Britain. Although we too have developed what has been described as the two thirds/one third society, I believe it well within the capabilities of Labour to develop policies for economic and social progress that can appeal to the contented majority.'[48] Elsewhere he has spoken of the need to 'target' benefits, the modern euphemism for means-testing, presumably one policy that would appeal to the 'contented majority'. Bryan Gould offered much of the same, referring to a 'time-warp' when Labour saw its role as 'offering help to a disadvantaged majority against a privileged

---

47. *Socialist Worker*, 25 April 1992.
48. *New Statesman*, 15 May 1992.

minority', which meant that 'we had little to say to those on middle incomes whose votes decides election . . . Nor did we make much effort to match the potent appeal of Tory policies on privatisation and council house sales.' He concludes: 'We ended up alienating one group of potential Labour voters by appearing to cap their aspirations, while failing to appeal to another group who were not impressed by our attempt to offer them greater benefits.'[49] Both urge a reconsideration of the nature of the links with the trade unions, embracing the idea of 'one member, one vote', and a growing if not explicit commitment to some form of proportional representation (incidentally a proposal in *Labour and the New Social Order* back in 1918).

The growing pressure to modify or even break the link with the unions has thrown its 'left' critics into something of a tizz, since it is their last figleaf of justification for supporting Labour. However, the unions are reverting much to what they were at the turn of the century, embracing only a minority of the working class, and its privileged sections at that. The new huge amalgamations – the AEU/EEPTU, Unison, the Civil Service Unions, the T&GWU or the G&MWU are private fiefdoms which depend on a secure income and an equally secure property portfolio running into hundreds of millions of pounds. They are now little more than the friendly benefit societies, offering cheap holidays, insurance, anything that requires the member to have a certain level of income. Provided the leaders can control the members – and these amalgamations have been structured with this in mind – then the empires will continue to accumulate even greater wealth. Because they cannot unite the interests of all sections of the working class as they could in the 1960s and 1970s, they can seek to organise only one – the new labour aristocracy. Hence such unions cannot represent the mass of the working class, and nor can the Labour Party which is based on them.

6.9 *Conclusion: the impending crisis*

British imperialism's decline is now rapid. As its creditor status comes

---

49. *ibid.*

to an end, the significance of the collapse of its industrial base will become increasingly apparent; together with the disappearance of North Sea oil revenues, it will contribute to increasingly severe balance of payments crises. Productivity may have risen, but only by 'sweating' existing assets, ie through making workers work harder and faster; it has not been as a result of new investment, which as we have mentioned, is below its 1979 level. Unemployment has now risen about a million over the past year; officially standing at 2.6 million, it is in reality of the order of 3.7 million.

Whilst investment in manufacturing fell, in the parasitic sectors it boomed: between 1979 and 1988, banking and finance investment rose 125.5 per cent, business services 148.4 per cent. Investment abroad also boomed: overseas direct investment amounted to 113 per cent of domestic manufacturing investment in 1980, 250 per cent in 1985, 370 per cent in 1989 and 164 per cent in 1990. But such figures were dwarfed by the volumes of portfolio investment and UK bank lending abroad: between 1980 and 1986, direct overseas investment totalled just over £46 billion, portfolio investment nearly £75 billion, and bank lending just over £200 billion. In other words, the most parasitic features of British imperialism came to the fore: it survived the 1980s by leeching off the rest of the world, either as a usurer – borrowing cheap and lending dear – or by exploiting cheap labour directly in countries such as South Africa.

With the advent of the 1990s, however, increasing inter-imperialist rivalries spelt the end of this privileged, parasitic existence, as the pressure from German and Japanese banking and finance capital took its toll. Fresh from setting aside £4 billion to cover bad debt in industry, the four major High Street banks are now also owed £12 billion by British property companies, which are in debt to the tune of £40 billion overall. There has been a slump in commercial property value of 40 per cent since 1990; the collapse of companies such as Speyhawk, Mountleigh and Olympia & York is but a taste of things to come. The fall in property values has rendered many companies technically insolvent, in the property sector as much as in manufacturing.

The accompanying deterioration in public services has been evident.

For the second successive year, the pupil-teacher ratio has risen after falling consistently for 25 years. This follows a fall in per capita spending on eduction of 2 per cent between 1980 and 1988, compared with a rise of 5 per cent in Germany, over 3 per cent in Italy and nearly 2 per cent in France. As a proportion of GDP, it fell from 5.5 per cent in 1980 to 4.5 per cent in 1990. The net volume increase in NHS expenditure fell by 1 per cent in the 1980s; its rise over the last two years reflects the cost of introducing the new reforms. Overall, between 1980 and 1989, health spending remained static at about 6 per cent of GDP, compared with 8.5 per cent in Germany in 1989, 8.8 per cent in France, 8 per cent in Italy and 6.5 per cent in Spain. State expenditure overall has fallen from 44.5 per cent of GDP in 1978-79 to 43 per cent in 1992/93; however, rising unemployment will continue to force it up – witness the growth in the estimated 1992/93 PSBR from £28 billion in autumn 1991 to about £34 billion in spring 1992. This includes an unprecedented deficit on the current revenue account of about £11 billion – borrowed not for capital projects, but to finance the tax cuts of the last years.

In these conditions, British imperialism can only sustain the privileged living standards of an ever-diminishing section of the working class, and then only at the expense of the mass, who will be condemned to increasing unemployment and poverty. The two thirds/one third society is moving towards a one half/one half society, and in the deepening crisis will become a one-third/two-thirds society. The Labour Party was formed by the privileged section of the working class to represent its interests and those of its middle class allies. Hence in conditions of crisis, it has stood against the interests of the mass of the working class, whether in the Empire or indeed at home. Whenever the working class and oppressed have fought to defend their interests, Labour has had no qualms at taking whatever steps have been necessary to suppress them. Labour has never advanced the cause of democracy or freedom one inch. It has never stood against imperialism and never stood against racism because the privileged conditions of the social stratum it represents depends on imperialism and depends on racism. This reality becomes more and more evident each time it counterposes the 'contented majority' to what it calls the 'underclass', that term of contempt for the oppressed working class which in itself reflects the corruption that is born of parasitism. Labour will not and cannot organise the ever-increasing poorer sections of the working class, and neither will its admirers on the left. History tells us, in the 1889 dockers' strike, the 1913 Dublin Lock-Out, the unemployed movement of the 1920s and 1930s, that it is only Marxists, revolutionaries and communists who can represent their interests. It will be no different in the future.

Bibliography

General histories:
Ralph Miliband, *Parliamentary Socialism*, 2nd Edition, Merlin Press 1972.
David Coates, *The Labour Party and the Struggle for Socialism*, Cambridge University Press, 1975.
James Hinton, *Labour and Socialism, A history of the British Labour Movement 1867-1974*, Harvester Press, 1983.
Tony Cliff and Donny Gluckstein: *The Labour Party: A Marxist History*, Bookmarks, 1988.
John Callaghan, *Socialism in Britain*, Blackwell, 1990.
Francis Williams, *Fifty Years' March: A History of the Labour Party*, Odhams Press, 1948.
Herbert Tracey, ed, *The British Labour Party*, 3 vols, Caxton, 1948. There is also a 1925 edition, *The Book of the Labour Party*.
Henry Pelling: *A Short History of the Labour Party*, 4th Edition, Macmillan, 1972.
GDH Cole and R Postgate, *The Common People*, Methuen, 1938.
AL Morton and G Tate, *The British Labour Movement*, Lawrence and Wishart, 1956.

On the early history of the Labour Party and the economics of the period:
Philip Poirier, *The Advent of the Labour Party*, George Allen and Unwin, 1958.
Theodore Rothstein, *From Chartism to Labourism*, Lawrence and Wishart, 1983.
S Pierson, *Marxism and The Origins of British Socialism*.
Ross McKibbin, *The Evolution of the Labour Party 1910-1924*.
Bernard Porter, *Critics of Empire: British Radical Attitudes to Imperialism in Africa 1895-1914*, Macmillan, 1966.
VI Lenin, *British Labour and British Imperialism*, Lawrence and Wishart, 1969.
RM Fox, *The Class Struggle In Britain*, 2 Vols, Martin Lawrence, circa 1930.
EJ Hobsbawm, *Industry and Empire*, Pelican, 1969; also his *Age of Empire 1875-1914*, Sphere Books, 1989.
David Reed: 'Marx and Engels on The Labour Aristocracy, Opportunism and British Labour Movement', *Fight Racism! Fight Imperialism!* No 27, March 1983.
Derek Aldcroft and Henry Richardson, *The British Economy 1870-1913*, Macmillan, 1969.
Dan Nabudere, *The Political Economy of Imperialism*, Zed Press, 1978.
Jurgen Kuczynski, *Labour Conditions under Industrial Capitalism*, Frederick Muller, 1972.

On the Labour Party and British imperialism in particular:
David Reed, *Ireland: Key to the British Revolution*, Larkin Publications, 1984.
R Fox, *The Colonial Policy of British Imperialism*, Martin Lawrence, circa 1933.
R Palme Dutt, *India Today*, Left Book Club, 1940.

R Palme Dutt, *The Crisis of Britain and the British Empire*, Lawrence & Wishart, 1953.

Brian Lapping, *End of Empire*, Granada Publishing, 1985.

PS Gupta, *Imperialism and the British Labour Movement 1914-64*, Cambridge, 1975.

S McIntyre, *Imperialism and the British Labour Movement in the 1920s*, Communist Party 'Our History' Pamphlet 64, 1975.

George Padmore, *Africa: Britain's Third Empire*, Dennis Dobson, 1949.

USSR Academy of Sciences, *A History of Africa 1918-67*, Nauka Publishing House, Moscow, 1968.

Articles from *Fight Racism! Fight Imperialism!*:

No 29 (May 1983): The Labour Party and Zionism (Steve Palmer); No 30 (June 1983): The Labour Party and South Africa (Carol Brown): No 31 (August 1983); The Labour Party and Viet Nam (Steve Palmer); No 32 (September 1983): The Labour Party and Kenya (Trevor Rayne & Eddie Abrahams); No 36 (February 1984): The Labour Party and Greece (Robert Clough); No 43 (October 1984): The Labour Party and South Yemen (Bill Hughes); No 99 (February/March 1991): The Labour Party and the Middle East (Robert Clough); No 103 (October/November 1991): The Labour Party and the Post-war Reconstruction of British Imperialism (Robert Clough).

On the economics of the more recent period:

P Bullock and D Yaffe: Inflation, The Crisis and The Post War Boom, *Revolutionary Communist* No 3/4, 1979.

On imperialism, racism and the split in the working class:

D Yaffe: 'Imperialism, National Oppression and the New Petit Bourgeoisie', and M Williams, S Palmer and G Clapton: 'Racism, Imperialism and the Working Class', both in *Revolutionary Communist* No 9, 1979; and *Manifesto of the Revolutionary Communist Group*, Larkin Publications, 1984.

On the Labour Party and the working class since 1918:

W Hannington: *Unemployed Struggles*, Lawrence and Wishart, 1977; *Ten Lean Years* Left Book Club.

Richard Croucher, *We Refuse to Starve in Silence*, Lawrence and Wishart, 1987.

Noreen Branson and Margot Heinemann, *Britain in the 1930s*, Granada, 1973.

Kenneth Morgan, *Labour in Power 1945-51*, Oxford University Press, 1986.

Paul Foot, *The Politics of Harold Wilson*, Penguin, 1968.

DN Pritt, *The Labour Government 1945-51*, Lawrence and Wishart, 1963.

R Ovendale, ed, *The Foreign Policy of the Labour Governments 1945-51*, Leicester University Press, 1984.

D Reed and O Adamson, *The Miners' Strike – People Versus State*, Larkin, 1985.

Index

subscribe

to the
best communist
anti-imperialist
newspaper in Britain
FIGHT RACISM!
FIGHT IMPERIALISM!

Subscription rates:
- [ ] Britain (inc. N. Ireland): £4.50 for six issues, £8 for 12 issues
- [ ] EC/Europe air printed paper rate: £6 for six issues, £11 for 12 issues
- [ ] EC/Europe air letter rate: £7 for 6 issues, £13 for 12 issues
- [ ] Africa, America, Middle East, South Asia – air printed paper rate
  £7.50 for 6 issues, £14 for 12 issues
- [ ] East Asia, Australasia, Pacific air printed paper rate: £8.50 for 6 issues,
  £16 for 12 issues.
- [ ] Libraries and institutions: double individual rates

Make cheques/POs payable to Larkin Publications. Add £5 for foreign currency cheques. Overseas rates are given for printed paper reduced rate and are unsealed. If you wish your mail to be sealed please let us know and we will inform you of the extra cost.

I would like to subscribe to Fight Racism! Fight Imperialism!

NAME_____

ADDRESS _____

_____

_____

I enclose payment of £ _____ for _____ issues at _____ rate

Return this form to: FRFI, BCM Box 5909, London WC1N 3XX